Herbs

Herbs

Essential know-how and expert advice for gardening success

CONTENTS

Planting a variety of pot-grown herbs, such as lavender, chives, sage, parsley, and thyme, is a particularly easy and effective way to start an herb garden.

WHY GROW HERBS?

Growing your own herbs is worthwhile, as well as being fun and easy to do. Herbs offer fabulous flavors and sensational scents, but they don't take much time, space, or trouble to grow. With just a little simple know-how, you can cultivate a broad range of beautiful as well as tasty and fragrant herbs in your garden or in your home, and use them in interesting ways. For very little effort, you can have all the well-known garden and supermarket staples within reach whenever you want, and you can boost your culinary prowess by trying more surprising plants and ingredients.

THE MOST USEFUL PLANTS

An herb is a plant with a purpose. We call any plant an herb if it is valued for its savory, sweet, aromatic, or health-promoting properties. They are the most versatile, multi-functional, and generous plants you can get, with a broad variety of flavors, scents, and characteristics. The leaves, flowers, stems, roots, and seeds of herbs have been used all over the world for thousands of years in many different pleasing and practical ways. These plants are grown to flavor food and drinks, and to make medicines, herbal remedies, fragrances, and home and beauty products. The more you use herbs, the more adventurous you will become with them.

TASTE SENSATION

Growing herbs to use in the kitchen when you cook and prepare food and drinks gives you the means to banish bland or boring meals from the table forever. Rosemary adds a depth of flavor to roasts, simple salads take on a new dimension with the addition of herb leaves and flowers, while drinks from teas to cordials come alive with the addition of fresh mint, lemon verbena, elderflower, or borage blooms. It's so satisfying to be able to add your own homemade *bouquet garni* to a stew, to use fresh basil leaves that you've just picked to make a pesto sauce, or to garnish a dish with chopped parsley that you have raised from seed.

When it comes to herbs, the only limit to what you can do is how daring you want to be. Growing your own herbs gives you the perfect opportunity to try new ideas and recipes with old favorites like dill or basil. Alternatively, you can try out new and exciting flavor combinations, take some risks, and experiment by growing and using herbs you might not be so familiar with, like hyssop, lovage, sweet cicely, Vietnamese coriander, or shiso.

Make your own fresh *bouquet garni* by tying together a bundle of herbs with string, and add them to soups and stews.

HELPFUL FOR HEALTH

As well as tasting great, herbs have been used throughout human history to aid and heal. These beneficial plants contain powerful chemical compounds that are still used today to create modern life-saving medicines, and make soothing essential oils and complementary health supplements.

By growing and using herbs you are also promoting your own good health, because they are an excellent way to add lots of flavor and bright, fresh color to food and drinks, both sweet or savory, thus helping you reduce your intake of salt and sugar. Many herbs are also rich in vitamins and minerals. Others have helpful properties to aid well-being, such as chamomile's calming effects and lavender's relaxing scent.

Many people find that the scent of lavender promotes a sense of relaxation and lessens feelings of anxiety.

Fennel seed is thought to alleviate indigestion and in some countries is offered for chewing at the end of a meal.

SUPER SCENT

One of the best things about herbs is the amazing aromas they exude. Brush past a block of hyssop beside a path, walk on a chamomile or thyme lawn, or rub the leaves of pineapple sage to release a fruity scent and you will understand the irresistible draw of these plants. Grow scented-leaf geraniums as house plants and they will bring fragrance to your home. Dry herbs to make potpourri, or use them in herb pillows to aid sleep or in drawer sachets to keep clothes smelling fresh and to deter insects. Use fennel or mint as a breath freshener, or mix a bunch of your favorites to draw a fragrant bath. There are so many ways to enjoy and take advantage of these aromatic superstars.

Bunches of herbs bring a welcome fragrance to the home.

Use the scented leaves and flowers of herbs to make potpourri for rooms and sachets to perfume clothes.

FREE AND FRESH

Home-grown herbs are fresher and so much tastier than store-bought cut herbs. They are also much more environmentally friendly, because your garden herb harvests come with zero food miles and no wasteful or plastic packaging. Buying a bunch of cut herbs at the supermarket can be expensive, but growing your own means you can often harvest again and again from the same plant, offering incredible value. And with good care and simple propagation you can have them year after year. Herbs are plants that just keep giving.

Nettles are herbs you may find for free in your yard. Once cooked, they become a delicious, sting-free vegetable.

RIPE AND READY

When you grow your own herbs, you can pick directly from the source and enjoy the freshest flavor. Instead of limp leaves from stores that would have been harvested days earlier, you'll be able to take advantage of having ripe herbs ready at your fingertips exactly when you want to use them. These fresh herbs will be better quality and taste so much better than what you can buy at the supermarket.

Growing your own also means you can enjoy herbs often only available to buy dried, such as bay leaves, straight from the plant. You may be surprised at how aromatic and delicious many of these fresh herbs are in comparison with their dried counterparts, and there is no danger of their being left in jars to grow musty.

TOP TIP PICKING LEAVES AND FLOWERS LITTLE AND OFTEN CAN INCREASE THE AMOUNT OF HERBS AVAILABLE TO YOU. PINCHING OUT THE SHOOTS AND TIPS WILL ENCOURAGE THE PLANT TO GROW MORE FOLIAGE.

Having herbs nearby to pick means they couldn't be fresher—mere minutes away from the stove or table.

SUSTAINABLE HARVESTS

Growing your own herbs is much more sustainable than buying them again and again. When you harvest at home, the only transporting required is your walk to cover the distance from the plant to the cooking pot or salad bowl, meaning no additional carbon emissions from delivery trucks, vans, or airplanes. There is no need for a bag or tray to package the herbs in, cutting down on plastic pollution, and by picking only the amount that you need, you will reduce food waste, instead of finding yourself having to throw away wilted, half-used packages of store-bought cut herbs from the fridge.

Herbs grown in your garden don't need packaging; they can be carried to the kitchen in any useful container.

YOUR CHOICE

We all want to make informed decisions about what we buy, eat, and use in our daily lives. When you cultivate your own herbs, you know precisely how they have been grown and what fertilizers or pest and disease control chemicals have been used. As well as this, you can try a more diverse range of herbs than just that available in stores, growing exciting plants that are difficult to source or not available in supermarkets, or choosing noteworthy cultivars of old favorites that offer more interesting aromas and flavors, and helpful attributes like drought tolerance or better resistance to bolting (flowering or setting seed too early).

Mint grows so easily in pots and in the garden that it needs no chemical help.

BETTER VALUE

It can be expensive to buy herbs, especially freshly cut and tropical varieties. Growing them yourself costs a lot less, and also ensures a steady supply that is abundant and renewable, because you can often harvest multiple times from the same herb plant.

As well as their leaves, many herbs have other parts—flowers, seeds, and roots—that you can use, many of which may not be widely available for sale or which would otherwise have to be bought separately, which isn't economical. You can also propagate your herb plants to make more plants for free, by sowing seed that you have collected, taking cuttings, or dividing established plants.

Fennel will produce plenty of seed to use as a spice or to grow new plants.

Taking rosemary cuttings is a good way of making new plants.

EASY GROW, ANYWHERE

Alongside their culinary and medicinal uses, herbs are also really beautiful garden plants in their own right, appealing to all the senses with their form, foliage, fragrance, and flowers. They are generally easy to grow, requiring next to no prior gardening experience or knowledge. Compared with other plants, cultivating herbs takes little time and effort, and they can be grown successfully almost anywhere, in gardens big and small, or—if you have no outdoor space—just on the kitchen windowsill. Every household can, and should, have as many herbs as possible.

SUPER SIMPLE

Herbs are so easy to grow that they are the perfect plants for beginners taking their first steps in growing their own edible plants. Fruit and vegetables can take knowledge, time, and space to grow well, but herbs are generally straightforward. Once you understand a few basics, you can get going right away, and will soon be enjoying tasty harvests. Growing herbs is simple enough for children, too—you can get the family involved, and delight together in nurturing and using these wonderful plants.

A collection of herbs that enjoy similar conditions can be grown together easily.

Herbs are easy and rewarding plants for children to grow.

LOW-MAINTENANCE

Modern lives are busy, and you may not have time available to tend to plants that need lots of care. All plants need some attention, often with regular watering and some feeding and weeding, but herbs are generally not demanding. Cut down on maintenance needs and resources by selecting the herbs that suit your particular growing conditions of soil and sunlight, so they don't require so much work. For example, in drier areas, choose drought-tolerant types like thyme or rosemary, so you don't have to constantly water them.

Herbs can be grown in the narrowest of containers on a sunny balcony or on a windowsill.

ANY SITUATION

Herbs come in many shapes and sizes, from small, leafy mounds to large, sturdy shrubs. They range from short-lived annuals like coriander that shine for just one season, to evergreens such as rosemary, which bring color and form to the garden all year. There are tender tropical plants that need to live indoors in cooler climates, and hardy ones that will brave the winter cold. This broad variety of herbs means that whatever your growing space, whether it's a pot in the kitchen, a window box, a few containers on the patio, or a large herb garden area, there are lots of suitable options to try.

NATURE'S BOUNTY

As well as offering an array of useful applications in the kitchen and home, herbs are beautiful garden plants that offer attractive structure and texture with their leaves and pretty, often scented, blooms. It's hard to beat the sight of a row of cheery purple chive flowers or a fragrant mass of blooming lavender. Many herbs are also known to attract beneficial insects including pollinators such as bees, butterflies, and hoverflies, while others are believed to repel pests. They can be used as companion plants to keep your whole garden healthy and happy.

The pretty globe heads and compact mound-forming habit of chives make them a highly decorative border plant.

HERBS FOR EVERY GARDEN

Herbs are so versatile that they can be grown in lots of different ways, and in any type of garden. Whatever your situation, there are inspirational ideas for how you can grow and get the most out of herbs. You can cultivate herbs easily in tiny spaces including window boxes and hanging baskets, or in pots on a balcony or patio. Enjoy evergreens in beds and borders all year, and colorful, edible flowers everywhere in summer. You can even make an entire lawn with fragrant herbs, or grow novel or rare tropical and tender herbs indoors as houseplants.

INDOOR HERBS

Growing your herbs indoors means they are always within arm's reach when you need them, and is a great way to maximize your growing area if you only have a tiny yard or balcony. It is also a perfect solution if you don't have any outdoor space at all.

Even for those with room outside, growing indoors means fresh herbs all year. Some plants will appreciate the warmth and shelter, and you have the chance to grow more tender, tropical plants that don't suit your garden's climate.

Many types of herb, including basil, sage, and thyme, will do well on a kitchen windowsill.

A clever hanging shelf unit for herbs makes the best use of light from a window.

WINDOWSILL HERBS

Several herbs are suitable for growing in pots on a kitchen windowsill, including annuals like basil and perennials such as mint and thyme. You can buy plants or sow from scratch, and simply pot up in an enriched potting mix and grow on as you would a plant in a container outside (see p.20). You can also lift herbs from the ground in the garden in early fall, divide them, and pot up to grow on through the winter indoors.

People often prefer to grow their indoor herbs in a plastic container with drainage holes, which they house inside a pretty display pot, so the plants look decorative while dirt and stains are kept to a minimum. Just remember to let the water drain out and empty the pot after watering so the herb's roots are not sitting in a wet puddle.

If you don't have a windowsill, try hanging your herb pots, or use a smart shelving solution to arrange lots of herb plants in one place.

A set of leaning shelves takes up little space for housing an array of herbs.

A **small indoor unit** with a growing light is a good way to raise herbs indoors if your access to natural light is limited.

Many ingredients for Thai curries can be grown indoors quite easily.

PERFECT SPOT

It is sensible to grow your herbs in the kitchen, where you need them, but first you should check if this is the best place to site them. Herbs grown indoors need sunlight, just like those outside, so the best spot is by a south-facing window where they will get at least six hours of bright light a day. Herbs will not thrive in the shade in the middle of a room, and will struggle in a shady north-facing window. There is also a lot less light available in winter. One solution is to use an electric grow light to give your herbs a boost. Give them good drainage, and keep them watered and fed just like your outdoor container herbs (see p.21), and they will reward you with many months' worth of bountiful pickings.

TROPICAL HOUSEPLANTS

There are several half-hardy and tender herbs from warm, hot, and humid places, including tropical and subtropical regions, that you can use to make tasty international dishes. Most of them will suffer and die in colder climates, but you can still grow herbs like stevia indoors, even if they are not suitable for your garden's conditions. You can also feel good knowing exactly where your food is coming from, and not have to worry about the air miles and carbon emissions it has cost to deliver the ginger from abroad for an Indian-inspired meal. Why not boost your interior style, as well as your range of fresh herbs, and make a themed culinary cluster of indoor herb pots? Then these beautiful herbs can spice up your dishes, and bring joy as health-boosting houseplants, too.

A particularly good selection to try would be a Thai curry container collection, including lemongrass, Thai lime, Thai basil, ginger, and coriander or Vietnamese coriander. All of these can be easily raised indoors—check the A–Z section (pp.60–141) on how to grow the individual plants.

COCKTAIL READY

If you know your mojito from your sangria, and love a summer gin and tonic that's heavy on the herbs, you'll want to make sure you have a supply of your favorite fresh ingredients on hand when it comes to cocktail time. As well as setting up your bar with booze and mixology tools, keep pots of herbs such as mint, basil, and rosemary in easy reach with a special indoor stash just for drinks. If you have no room for a proper bar, an ingenious solution is a bar cart, which can be kept in a sunny spot for the plants when it's not needed, then wheeled over to where you want to mix the drinks when you're ready to make a cocktail or two.

A bar cart with indoor plants and herbs is decorative and practical.

HERBS FOR TINY SPACES

When growing space is at a premium, you need plants that deliver maximum value and enjoyment in a small package. Herbs are a great choice because they provide foliage, flowers, and fragrance, as well as flavor in the kitchen. Grouping herbs in containers—from old tin cans to hanging baskets—will transform the smallest balcony, patio, or even window ledge into a productive mini garden. Key to success is a sunny spot: a few herbs will grow in shade, but most require plenty of light.

MINI MARVELS

Some herbs are well suited to growing in tight spaces. Avoid shrubby evergreen perennials like rosemary, or parsley with its long tap root. Choose annual herbs such as basil and coriander, which don't need much growing space. Shallow-rooting herbs such as thyme and drought-tolerant ones like sage are also good bets. Dwarf or compact cultivars are particularly space-efficient.

COMPACT CULTIVARS TO TRY Basil 'Greek', 'Aristotle', 'Emily', or 'Puck' • Dill 'Fern Leaf' or 'Nano' • Oregano 'Compactum' • Sage 'Compacta'

Upcycled cans make decorative containers for these mint plants.

A hanging planter with pockets for herbs is simple to affix to a wall and makes effective use of minimal space.

A vertical planter made from an old wooden pallet has a small footprint and can hold numerous herb plants.

GROWING UP

Treat limited outdoor space as a creative challenge. If you have a long, thin alley or patio, choose a elongated container, such as a watering trough. Don't be afraid of planting against a fence or wall (as long as there is sufficient light) as this will help keep plants warm and sheltered.

If you have little or no room outside, try greening up fences and railings with saddlebag planters that hang over each side, or buy a hanging wall planter, which is studded with pockets that can each be planted with a different herb. Free-standing vertical planters also take up little space. They can be bought in various sizes and you can even make your own by recycling a wooden pallet. To do this, first pull out or hammer in any sharp nails in the pallet and sand down all rough edges. Attach pieces of weed-control membrane to the front and back slats with a staple gun to create planting pockets. Fill the pockets with potting mix and your chosen herbs.

A WINDOWSILL GARDEN

For herbs to pick whenever they are needed, plant up a container for your windowsill. You can buy a ready-made planter or make your own (see below). Either way, it must have drainage holes in its base and be placed in a stable position on the sill.

1 Put some crocks or broken pottery in the bottom of the container, over the drainage holes. These still allow water to drain but prevent potting mix from leaking out.

2 Half-fill the container with potting mix. It's worth mixing in granules of water-retaining gel (available from your garden center), following the instructions on the packet, to reduce the frequency with which you need to water.

3 Add the plants, gently squeezing them in around each other. Top up with potting mix, ensuring all the gaps and holes are filled, and firm down around the plants with your fingers.

4 Make sure the container is stable on the window ledge, or securely affixed to it, and keep it well watered.

TOP TIP IF YOU CAN, SITE YOUR BOX BY A SOUTH-FACING WINDOW, UNDER THE EAVES: THIS PREVENTS SOIL BEING WASHED AWAY BY HEAVY RAINS.

Cheap and colorful, planters made from juice cartons are a hit with kids.

Use annual herbs to plant in cartons; neither will last longer than one season.

SHORT-TERM SOLUTIONS

To save money and help the environment, make window planters from old, waxed juice cartons. Cut the top third off with scissors, and wash out the inside. Punch drainage holes in the bottom with a pen. Link several cartons together with paper clips, and plant up as above.

To get the best value from your herbs, cut the new growth often and use it in your cooking. New, juicy growth will come back quickly, and you'll prevent the plant from becoming too "leggy," prolonging its useful life.

HERBS IN CONTAINERS

Most herbs will grow readily in containers if they are given the right care and consideration. Growing in pots is the perfect option for those who have a small yard or no ground beds, or for those who want to have their favorite, most-used herbs a few short steps away on the patio. Containers offer the chance to grow herbs that need a different soil pH and drainage than what you naturally have, and they are helpful for growing less hardy herbs that need to be brought under cover for the winter.

A collection of herbs in pots by the back door makes it quick and easy to pick them when they are wanted.

PLANTING UP POTS

You can grow herbs in any container, from a terra-cotta pot or a lined basket or crate to an old metal washtub or wheelbarrow. Whatever you choose, use containers that have drainage holes at the bottom, because good drainage is essential. You may be able to drill or use a nail and hammer to create some if necessary. Pop a few pieces of broken pottery, called crocks, in the base so the potting mix doesn't drain out of the bottom or clog up the hole.

Container herbs need a very well-drained, light growing medium. The best is commercial potting mix enriched with the addition of organic matter such as compost, and added perlite for drainage. Mix three parts potting mix with one part sand or composted fine bark to improve drainage. You can also add some water-holding gel, following the manufacturers' instructions on the package, to prevent the mix drying out too quickly in the summer.

Part-fill your container with the growing mix, and add your herbs

without cramming them. Fill in with more mix and firm in, leaving a gap of at least ½ in (2 cm) from the top of the pot. Water well, and place in a spot that satisfies the plants' light requirements.

You can also sow seed direct into containers in spring once all risk of frost has passed.

Recycle plastic tubs or buckets as herb containers by drilling drainage holes.

Gently firm the potting mix in the container around newly planted thyme.

Scented-leaf geraniums need bringing indoors in winter, so are perfect for pots.

CONTAINER CARE

Herbs grown in pots need more regular watering during the growing season than those grown in the ground, because there is such a small amount of soil in the container and it dries out much more quickly. In warm weather, you may have to water your herb pots every day. You will also have to feed pot-grown herbs occasionally, because they don't have easy access to a supply of nutrients. Choose a balanced liquid fertilizer, which will encourage leafy growth rather than flowers. Follow the instructions on the label, using it throughout the growing season but, for best flavor, feeding slightly less often than recommended. Remember to use a feed that is suitable for edible plants.

Mint can be invasive grown in the ground, so it is often best to confine it to a pot.

BEST HERBS FOR CONTAINERS

Basil • Bay • Chives • Coriander • Lemon verbena • Lovage • Mint • Oregano • Parsley • Rosemary • Sage • Savory • Scented-leaf geranium • Sorrel • Tarragon • Thyme • Vietnamese coriander • Wasabi

Grouping together your herb pots, vegetable, and salad plants will make watering and feeding them easier.

WINTER WORRIES

Many perennial herbs that originate from the Mediterranean, such as lavender, thyme, sage, savory, and rosemary, hate exposed, wet conditions in winter. It's a good idea to put your containers on pot feet or lift them up on bricks so they can drain properly at the bottom, or the herbs may rot off. Reduce watering to a minimum from fall to spring.

Herbs in pots are also more likely to be damaged by cold weather, because their roots are out of the ground, and not so well insulated. You can protect them in frosty or icy conditions by moving them to the shelter of a house wall, and wrapping the container in horticultural fleece or bubble wrap.

Horticultural fleece is good for protecting plants when cold is forecast.

Raising pots off the ground on pot feet will ensure good drainage.

HERBS IN THE GARDEN

If you have room and soil to grow herbs in the ground, you can look forward to lots of bounteous harvests and a beautiful, fragrant garden to boot. Check on your natural microclimate and conditions, including light, and group herbs that have similar needs together to keep them happy and make their care and maintenance easier for you. Alternatively, you can spread them out throughout the space to brighten up every corner with foliage, flower, and fragrance. Once you know your options, there are plenty of ingenious ways to grow herbs in your garden.

Herbs can be mixed with flowers and vegetables for an informal look.

HERB GARDENS

Growing herbs in their own exclusive area, whether that's a whole herb garden or a dedicated bed or border, makes harvesting easy and will look and smell wonderful. You could design themed sections, such as an edible flower bed, a potpourri border, or a culinary collection with all your favorites for the kitchen in one spot. Herbs are often grown alongside fruit and vegetables in kitchen gardens and allotments, planted between rows or providing a wonderful low edging. This is called intercropping, making the most of every inch of soil and keeping weeds down, or companion planting when used to attract beneficial insects and keep away pests.

Lavish planting of lavender and thyme surrounds a lovely scented seating area.

BEDS AND BORDERS

If you don't have space to dedicate solely to herbs, they are just as happy planted in other areas all over the garden, including in your ornamental borders and beds. Planted alongside flowers and shrubs, herbs give form, texture, and color. You can bring welcome height at the back with tall fennel or valerian, or create low mounds to fill the front of the border with oregano. You can fill summer gaps with pretty blooms like feverfew and cornflowers, or create bright foliage interest with silvery wormwood and sage. All this, plus their scent and flavor, makes herbs indispensable plants that you should have in every nook and cranny you can fit them in.

Rows of herbs growing together in regimented rows make a striking pattern in a formal herb garden.

Having herbs growing in raised beds makes them easier to access for planting, care, and harvesting.

Raised beds provide attractive settings for herbs in an otherwise paved space.

RAISED BEDS

Raised beds are a great way to grow herbs if you don't have ideal soil conditions or it is difficult for you to access ground beds. Essentially, you build a frame to lift the bed out of the ground by anything from 4–39 in (20–100 cm), and fill it with your choice of soil. This gives you many more opportunities. If you have, for example, clay soil, a raised bed provides you with the chance to import light, sandy loam topsoil so you can grow Mediterranean herbs like lavender, rosemary, and basil that prefer good drainage. They are an excellent choice for those with restricted mobility, because they raise the herbs up and reduce the need to bend over, making it easier to plant, maintain, and harvest.

Raised beds are also much larger than containers and pots, so they don't require as much attention such as watering and feeding. They are usually made from timber, but also brick and, increasingly, metal. Avoid using railroad crossties that have been treated with creosote, and use a plastic liner if growing edible plants in a steel bed to prevent zinc leaching out.

Lavender makes a beautiful edging to a path and will release a wonderful fragrance as you brush past it.

PERFECT PLACES

You will find lots of situations where herbs can be used to advantage in your garden. Line a path with rows of lavender for a scented summer walk by clouds of purple flowers, or use the pretty mauve flower heads of chives to make a low edging for a border. You can make an herb lawn, walk, or seat with chamomile (see p.24), or brighten bare, dry areas with flowering thymes.

Evergreen herbs can offer structure and interest all year. Use rosemary to make a low hedge, or clip bay into a topiary cone or pyramid to create an attractive focal point that looks green and neat even through winter. Even that scrubby problem spot in the shade can be solved with an herb like sweet woodruff, which makes a magnificent ground cover.

HERBS FOR GROUND COVER

Herbs are a great ground cover alternative to grass lawns, providing a low, green carpet that does not need to be constantly mowed. They can also be used in awkward areas, such as sloping banks and gaps in paving, where it would be difficult to mow. They will keep weeds down and offer the extra benefit of exciting aromas when touched or walked on. Some also have the bonus of pretty, colorful flowers.

Corsican mint (*Mentha requienii*) is a small-leaved, shade-loving mint that can spread to form an aromatic carpet.

SCENTED SWATHES

An herb lawn or path is a beautiful and fragrant feature for any garden. They are most commonly made with chamomile or creeping thymes. Even though it doesn't flower, lawn chamomile 'Treneague' is the best choice, as it forms a low mat just 2½–4 in (5–10 cm) high. It does not grow from seed, so buy small plants or plugs to start; they are often available in large pack sizes expressly for making lawns. You will need around 50 chamomile plugs per 10 sq ft (1 sq meter), spaced 6–8 in (15–20 cm) apart,

but you can plant them more closely for quicker coverage, at up to 100 per 10 sq ft (1 sq meter), spaced 4 in (10 cm) apart. For a thyme lawn, you will need about 36 small plants per 10 sq ft (1 sq meter), spaced around 6 in (15 cm) apart.

Choose a spot in full sun, which has light or occasional rather than constant heavy foot traffic. The soil should be light and well-drained. A sandy loam is preferable, and heavier or clay soils should be avoided or improved with sand and organic matter such as well-rotted compost. Remove all weeds from the area, and dig over the soil to a spade's

depth, removing any stones or roots, before raking over to level the surface.

For best results, plant plugs in spring, once all risk of frost has passed. Use a dibble to make a small, deep hole for each plug. Pop in the plug and gently firm the soil back around it with your hands. Work from a plank of wood laid across the space to prevent compacting the soil as you go. Water in well once you are finished, and keep the soil moist for the first few weeks, and during dry periods while the plants establish. Weed the area meticulously by hand, keeping the soil around the plants clear, and don't walk on it for at least three months. Keep foot traffic very light for the first year.

Once established, trim chamomile in late summer, and thyme after flowering, with hand shears, to keep growth vigorous and a neat form.

A whole herb lawn is ambitious, but many gardeners choose to have a small herb "welcome mat" or path instead. The process is exactly the same as for a lawn, but in a smaller space. In a similar way, you can create a chamomile or thyme bench or seat, by using a sturdy planter, small raised bed, or other structure—just make sure you have at least 4 in (10 cm) depth of soil for the plants to grow in, and fill it to the brim.

Different flowering thymes make a tapestry-like herb lawn.

A small chamomile path can be easier to create than a whole lawn.

CRACKS AND GAPS

Squeeze plants into every nook and cranny in your garden by using herbs between pavers on your patio or stepping stones in a path, so you release wafts of sumptuous scent as you walk along. Perennial and evergreen, low spreading and creeping thymes are fantastic at bringing these little gaps and cracks to life. Choose one cultivar for a uniform and dramatic display when the flowers appear, or make an interesting tapestry effect by mixing types with different colors of flower and foliage.

1 Split up individual plants to make smaller pieces, either by pulling the plant apart, or cutting down through the root ball with a knife to make three or four sections, each with top growth, soil, and roots.
2 Dig out the cracks or gaps and squeeze in the plants. Space them evenly and fill back in and around them with compost if necessary.
3 Water in well and keep watered for the first few weeks, and in dry periods while the plants establish.
4 Trim back closely with hand shears after flowering, and trim again in the fall if plants are looking straggly, to keep them neat.

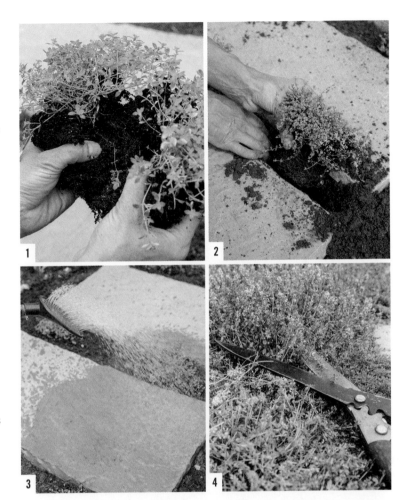

TOP GROUND COVER HERBS

Perfect plants for herb lawns, paths, and seats, and also for covering awkward areas, include:

FOR SUN
Chamomile 'Treneague' or double-flowered 'Flore Pleno' • Prostrate rosemary • Thyme 'Bressingham', Coccineus Group, 'Doone Valley', 'Pink Chintz', or 'Snowdrift'

FOR SHADE
Corsican mint • Sweet woodruff

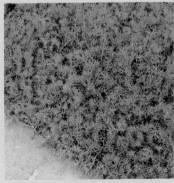

Lawn chamomile (*Chamaemelum nobile* 'Treneague') thrives in sun.

Sweet woodruff (*Galium odoratum*) prefers to grow in shade.

All herbs will need watering regularly when newly planted, but many are tolerant of dry conditions once they are well established.

GROWING HERBS

Herbs are not difficult to grow. Simply give them the right conditions and a little care and attention, and they will reward you with abundant harvests all season long. In this section, you will find a straightforward guide on how to cultivate all sorts of herbs—evergreen and deciduous, annual and perennial—in different garden situations. Learn how to sow and plant herbs, and the best ways to care for them. There is also advice on how to propagate more herb plants for free, and there are troubleshooting tips for common problems.

HERB LIFE CYCLES

Many different types of plant are used as herbs, and they have a broad range of characteristics and growth habits. There are annual herbs, like basil and coriander, which only last for one growing season. Perennial herbs, like mint and tarragon, die back above ground over the winter, but revive each spring with fresh growth. Then there are herbs like rosemary and sage, which are evergreens that keep their leaves throughout the winter, giving interest to the garden throughout the colder months.

Chervil is a biennial that is usually grown as an annual. If left for a second year, it will regrow, flower, and set seed, and then die back for good.

Annual herbs like coriander need to be sown fresh each season.

Dill is an annual that can be left to flower and self-seed in the garden.

ANNUALS AND BIENNIALS

Annual herbs live for just one growing season. This means that they need to be sown and grown from scratch each year, and replaced the following year. They can be harvested all summer up until the first frosts, when they will begin to die back. Many annual herbs, like dill and coriander, will produce seed if left to flower at the end of the season. You can collect this seed to sow next year, or you can simply allow the plant to self-seed onto the soil, which will result in lots of little seedlings coming up in the following spring.

Biennial herbs need two years to complete their life cycle. They produce leaves in their first season, followed by flowers and leaves in their second season, and then die. Biennial herbs grown for their leaves, such as parsley and chervil, are usually treated like annuals, and freshly sown every year. Those grown for flowers, such as chicory, are left to regrow in their second year.

Parsley is a biennial that produces dense foliage in its first year. You can cover it with a cold frame in winter and pick leaves through to the following spring.

Mint is a deciduous perennial that dies back over winter, returning in spring.

Evergreen bay leaves can be harvested all year.

Catmint is a perennial that is often grown to repel insects.

Basil is an annual that grows fast from seed in a few months.

Lavender is a fragrant perennial, often grown for structure and color.

Semi-evergreen winter savory is a low-maintenance herb.

TYPES OF HERB

POPULAR ANNUALS
Arugula (salad) • Basil • Borage • Coriander • Dill • Nasturtium • Pot marigold • Scented leaf geranium • Summer savory

POPULAR BIENNIALS
Caraway • Celery leaf • Chervil • Milk thistle • Parsley

POPULAR DECIDUOUS PERENNIALS
Arugula (wild) • Bee balm • Catmint • Chamomile • Chives • Fennel • Feverfew • Lovage • Marjoram • Mint • Oregano • Rue • Sorrel • Sweet cicely • Sweet woodruff • Tarragon • Valerian

POPULAR EVERGREEN PERENNIALS
Bay • Cotton lavender • Hyssop • Lavender • Rosemary • Sage • Thyme

PERENNIAL HERBS

Deciduous perennial herbs live for several years, offering season after season of fresh pickings. Their foliage may die back over the winter, but new growth returns in the spring.

Evergreen perennial herbs, which stay green all winter, typically have woody stems and shrubby forms. They provide great value because, in addition to their culinary uses, they are often ornamental, providing structure and color when there is very little else going on in the garden. Some can be trained into topiary shapes (bay, for example, is often shaped into cones) or used as informal hedging (rows of clipped lavender make effective and pretty boundaries). Many perennial herbs, including rosemary, can be picked for culinary use all year, although their growth does slow considerably in lower winter temperatures. Chives can behave like evergreens in mild areas.

A third class of perennial herbs, such as wormwood and winter savory, are "subshrubs." These are semi-evergreen; they don't always lose their leaves in winter, so you can keep harvesting them, but remain "resting" without putting on any new growth, so they can resume growing quickly when the conditions get warmer. However, in cold winters, they may lose their leaves entirely.

SOWING AND GROWING FROM SEED

There is something almost magical about sprinkling some seeds onto soil, and waiting with anticipation for the delicate shoots to emerge and grow on to become plants. The process of seedlings sprouting from seed is called germination, and it usually requires warmth, water, and air—how much of each depends on the plant. Many herbs can be grown from seed, and starting herbs off like this, whether sowing indoors or directly in the ground outside, is a cheap and fulfilling way to produce lots of luscious herb plants.

GOING UNDER COVER

If you want to jump-start your growing season, you can sow seed in early spring. However, the majority of seedlings will be killed off by a cold spell outdoors at this time of year, so it is advisable to start things off under cover instead. This means sowing seeds into trays, plug modules, or pots of seed starting mix and germinating them indoors, in a warm, light place such as a greenhouse, polytunnel, conservatory, or even a bright windowsill. Sowing under cover is particularly useful for herbs that might need special conditions or a little more attention to germinate. For example, basil will not germinate in cold soil.

Seeds are sold in waterproof, airtight packets. Check the use-by date on the pack—you can still sow out-of-date seeds, but they are less likely to germinate. Clean and dry your trays or pots and fill with seed starting mix. Don't use any other mix, as it will have too many nutrients, or garden soil, which may be heavy, lumpy, and full of weeds.

Large seeds are usually pushed into the growing mix a little and then covered over with more mix. Medium-size seeds can be pressed gently into the surface and covered very lightly, while tiny seeds can be scattered across the surface. These very small seeds are most likely to need light to germinate, so should not be covered. Herbs that don't like their roots being disturbed should be sown in plug modules or pots, so they can develop a good root ball without interruption from pricking out. This is ideal for plants that develop tap (large, central) roots or have a habit of bolting early. Water gently with a watering can with a fine rose, so you don't wash the seeds away. Let the water drain through. For very fine seed, you can set the tray or pot in a container of water, or moisten the growing mix before sowing.

Place the trays or pots where they have lots of light, but not direct sun. Some herbs will benefit from the warmth provided by a propagator—a seed tray with a fitted lid. You can also use an electric one that gives extra heat from the base; when sprouts appear, turn off the heat.

You may find it easiest to start with a few seeds in the palm of your hand.

Sprinkle the seeds onto seed starting mix in plugs, trays, or pots.

A propagator with a lid provides seeds with an even, warm temperature.

Always hold seedlings by a leaf, not the more easily damaged stem.

PRICKING OUT

After they have sprouted, the seedlings in your tray will often be growing very close together in a cluster. They will produce a first set of little leaves, called seed or cotyledon leaves, and then true leaves, which look like smaller versions of the leaf shape typical for that herb. When the seedlings have 3–4 true leaves, and are large enough to handle, they can be "pricked out"—gently transplanted to a larger growing space, such as their own individual modules or pots, to grow on.

Prepare the modules or pots with fresh potting mix. Take a dibble (a pointed sticklike tool), a pencil, or old fork, and make a small hole in the potting mix. Holding the seedling by its leaf—never the stem—use the dibble to gently loosen its roots from the soil. Lift it out of the tray carefully, and lower down into the hole in its new pot, teasing the roots in with the dibble. Make sure the seedling is resting at the same level it was growing previously, and firm in the potting mix around the roots and base.

Water in and continue growing the seedlings on under cover until all risk of frost has passed. At this time, watch for damping off, a fungal disease that can destroy seedlings (see p.43).

Seedlings can take from a few days to several weeks to sprout.

SOWING DIRECT

Once the weather warms up (usually in mid- to late spring) and there is less risk of a sudden frost that would kill tender young plants, you can sow seed of many herbs direct into the ground where they are to grow. First, see what type of soil you have (see p.33) and check on the herb you want to grow in the A–Z (see pp.60–141) to see if this is suitable; if it requires a well-drained neutral soil, it probably won't germinate or grow in damp, heavy clay. If your soil isn't right, you can sow direct onto the surface of a container of potting mix instead.

Prepare the soil by digging it over to break it up to a workable, finer texture. Remove all weeds and any rocks or stones, and rake the surface smooth. If you wish to grow herbs in a row, peg a line of string and use a bamboo cane in the soil to follow the straight line and create a shallow drill (sowing channel). Alternatively, make several small holes with a dibble where you want the herbs to grow. Sow your seeds along the row, or in clusters in the small holes, cover lightly with soil using the rake, and water with a fine rose on the watering can or hose.

Once they have germinated and the seedlings have developed several true leaves, you can thin them out. This means removing some of the seedlings to give the healthiest ones more space and the best chance of growing strong. Simply pluck the unwanted ones from the soil and discard, or use the leaves as microgreens. Watch out for slugs and snails, and protect with horticultural fleece or a cloche if frost is forecast.

> **TOP TIP** SOME ANNUAL HERBS, SUCH AS CORIANDER OR ARUGULA, CAN BOLT (RUN TO FLOWER) QUICKLY, ESPECIALLY IN HOT WEATHER OR DRY SOIL. THIS MAKES THEIR LEAVES TOUGH OR BITTER. TO ENSURE A STEADY SUPPLY OF THE BEST, FRESHEST LEAVES ALL SEASON, SOW SUCCESSIONALLY—A FEW SEEDS EVERY TWO WEEKS—SO YOU CAN KEEP ON HARVESTING.

To make a row of herbs, sow along a narrow, shallow trench (known as a drill).

CHOOSING AND PLANTING HERB PLANTS

Some herbs are challenging to germinate, and others take a long time to produce a harvest from seed. Buy these herbs as ready-grown plugs or potted plants. Choose healthy specimens and plant them in the spot with the most suitable conditions to give them a good start. The best time to buy and plant herbs is in spring, but many perennial and shrubby herbs can also be planted in the fall.

Basil plants should be well spaced and watered when planted out in the garden.

SELECTING GOOD PLANTS

If you are shopping in a garden center or nursery, there are a few things to keep in mind to make sure you buy healthy herb plants. Look at the leaves: are they yellow, brown, or wilting? Are there weeds on the surface of the soil? Good-quality plants will be lush, green, and weed- and moss-free. Check the bottom of the pot: are there lots of roots coming out of the bottom? This may indicate that the herb has been in its container for too long and is pot-bound, so won't perform well.

When buying herbs online or by mail order, make sure you understand the size of the plant you are ordering. As soon as they arrive, unpack and check them over. Contact the company immediately if there's a problem. The best way to avoid issues is to choose suppliers who are recommended and respected in the industry and well reviewed by customers.

> **TOP TIP** DON'T PLANT IN SUMMER WHEN IT'S WARM AND DRY, UNLESS YOU CAN WATER THE PLANTS ALL THE TIME TO HELP THEM ESTABLISH.

Healthy herbs for sale should have fresh, unblemished foliage.

HERB PLUGS

Plug plants are small, young plants or seedlings that have been grown in a module, so they have a soil plug and roots, but no pot. You should plant your herb plugs as soon as you can. Take them out of the packaging, pot up individually in potting mix, and water in. These baby herbs will probably not be hardy, and so should be grown on under cover indoors until they have almost filled the pot with their roots, and there is no longer a risk of a frost outdoors—usually late spring.

When seedlings have filled their pot, plant them on, first teasing out the roots.

HARDENING OFF

Before you plant your sown seedlings or bought plug plants outside in the garden, they have to go through a process of conditioning known as hardening off, to prepare them for the change in temperature and exposure between indoors and outdoors. Once all risk of frost has passed in spring, place the plants outside during the day and bring them back under cover overnight, for around 10–14 days. After this, they should be ready to get planted out in the ground or outside in pots.

Bring plants grown under cover outside in the day for a week or two.

THE RIGHT CONDITIONS

When planting any herb, first check the A–Z section (see pp.60–141) as to what conditions it prefers, including light and drainage requirements and soil type. Many herbs come from warm, dry regions such as the Mediterranean, and like a light or sandy, well-drained soil in full sun. They are not likely to thrive in shade in a heavy, wet soil. You will get the best results by planting herbs in the right place to suit their needs.

Check your soil texture—is it sticky to the touch when handled like clay, or gritty like sand? Free-draining sandy soils don't tend to hold on to nutrients, so are poor in fertility, while clay soils can be rich in nutrients but retain water, which can contribute to root rot and kill herbs in winter. There are also soil testing kits available that can tell you if your soil is alkaline, neutral, or acidic.

Whatever you discover, you can improve your soil with the addition of organic matter such as well-rotted manure or garden compost, but if it is completely unsuitable for the herbs you want to grow, plant them in containers.

Even if the plant is not pot-bound, tease out the roots when planting out.

Press down the soil around the new plant to firm it in.

Clay soil will be tacky and clumpy in texture, sticking together when pressed.

PLANTING HERBS

To plant a potted herb out in the garden, you first have to prepare the ground. Clear the area of weeds, stones, and large clumps of soil. Using a spade or trowel, dig a hole that is slightly deeper and wider than the pot. Pile the soil nearby. Pop the herb plant out of the pot. Tease some of the roots out from the mass at the base of the root ball. Place in the hole, checking that the surface of the root ball is level with the top of the hole. Pull the heaped soil back into the hole with your hands to fill in the gap around the plant, breaking up any clumps and firming the soil in to ensure there are no air gaps. Water well.

CARING FOR HERBS

Herbs are low-maintenance plants that don't require much fuss or attention. They do, however, offer fresh pickings all through the season, and will stay lush and green and continually provide tasty harvests if you give them just a modicum of care. Maintaining the health and productivity of your herbs is easy and well worth the extra effort—good cultivation is simply about mastering a few growing basics.

WATERING

Even drought-tolerant herbs, such as thyme and lavender, need to be watered regularly in their first season after planting. Once established, they might only need water in dry spells, but leafy herbs such as dill, arugula, and cilantro may bolt if dry, so need consistent irrigation to help prevent this. Push your finger into the soil near the base of the plant to check if there is moisture beneath the surface. Water in the morning if you can—this helps the herbs take up more water and lowers the risk of pests and diseases—and always water the soil around the plant and not its leaves, as this could lead to scorch and fungal issues.

It is better to give a good soak to plants growing in the ground once a week or every few days than to water them a little every day. The exception to this is herbs growing in containers. Because they only have a small amount of soil to grow in, they dry out quickly, so need more watering—daily in warm summer weather.

Herbs in pots need more feeding and watering than ground-growing ones.

FEEDING

If your herbs are planted in the right conditions with their preferred soil fertility, they may not need any additional feeding, but to help those herbs that will benefit from a boost in nutrition, such as those grown in pots and perennial herbs that come back every year, you can apply a general-purpose liquid fertilizer that is designed especially for edible plants during the growing season, following the instructions on the pack. Alternatively, you can use liquid seaweed feed or make your own compost tea with comfrey (see p.128) or nettles. Apply any fertilizer around the base of the plant, not on the leaves.

All newly planted herbs need to be thoroughly and regularly watered while they are establishing.

TOP TIP HERBS WILL NOT GROW WELL WHEN THEY ARE IN COMPETITION WITH WEEDS AND OTHER PLANTS THAT MUSCLE IN TO TAKE UP THEIR SPACE, LIGHT, AND NUTRIENTS, SO SPACE PLANTS THE RECOMMENDED DISTANCE APART AND KEEP THE AREA AROUND THEM CLEAR OF WEEDS.

MULCHING

A mulch is a covering around the base of a plant that can help keep the soil moist by preventing evaporation, offer extra protection from the cold over winter, and keep weeds down by stopping their germination by blocking the light from

Apply leaf mold as a nutritious mulch around herbs growing in the ground.

getting to them. Organic mulches such as garden compost or well-rotted manure can also help replenish fertility by adding nutrients to the soil. Other organic mulches include leaf mold and composted straw. Inorganic mulches include gravel, which is ideal for Mediterranean herbs like thyme which prefer good drainage. Apply a good layer of mulch around the plant. A typical depth is ½–2 in (2–5 cm).

PRUNING

Herbs that are harvested regularly will usually stay vigorous in growth and neat in shape, but even these plants will need cutting back at some point in their growth cycle to be at their best.

As a first step, when your young herbs have been planted out in the garden, whether in the ground or in pots, and start to put on growth, it's a good idea to "pinch out" the growing tips by simply snipping them off between your finger and thumb just above the next set of leaves. This will promote side shoots to

grow and encourage the plant to branch into a bushier shape and promote fuller, leafier plants.

Most leafy herbs are best harvested before they flower, so also snip out or deadhead any flower stems that you see forming to prolong productive growth. Once plants have flowered, deadhead to prevent self-seeding, or just cut the whole plant back to encourage a fresh flush of leaves and, for herbs such as lavender, to retain a compact shape.

Annuals such as basil and coriander can be lifted and discarded on the compost heap once they have started to

die back at the end of the season. Hardy deciduous perennial herbs such as mint can be left in situ. You can cut the old stems down once the top growth has died back in fall, or leave them up until spring, but make sure to remove dead foliage or detritus around the base of the plant before winter.

Evergreens like rosemary can get leggy and bare at the base without regular pruning. Clip back in spring to just above where the last season's growth began, where you can see fresh buds or leaves forming—never cut into old wood, or the plant may not recover.

Pinch out the soft new growing tips of sage to promote a bushy, full shape. Older plants may also need cutting back in spring.

Lavender needs to be clipped back after flowering to keep its shape.

STORE-BOUGHT HERB HACKS

In stores and supermarkets you may see lots of fresh herbs—cut stems, plants growing in pots, or seeds in little jars—and wonder if they will grow. The good news is that, with a little effort, many of them will, and you can have fun trying out an array of store-bought goodies to see what will grow, root, and sprout. It is exciting to experiment with a supermarket pot, or what you already have in your spice rack or tea caddy, or have left over in a packet of fresh herbs from dinner last night.

A pencil or dibble can help to gently tease the plants apart.

Replant each separated herb plant into fresh potting mix.

PACKED POT PLANTS

It's common to find small pots of herbs available in the supermarket as well as cut herbs. These pots are crammed with many little plants—grown from really densely sown seed in potting mix with little nutrition—and the intense competition for water, nutrients, and light with so many seedlings in that tiny space is why these plants never seem to last very long on your kitchen windowsill.

You can, however, give them a better chance of survival by splitting these packed pots up into individual plants or smaller clumps, and potting on into fresh potting mix in other containers. This idea is most successful with annual leafy green herbs like basil and cilantro, but you can try it with others such as parsley, rosemary, thyme, sage, and chives, too.

Soak the pot in water for a few minutes, and then ease the root ball out of the pot. Place it down on a flat surface and gently separate out the seedlings or clumps from each other—to begin with, it may help to use a dibble or pencil to ease them apart. Transplant each plant or small clump into a new pot filled with fresh potting mix, placing it at the same level it was growing before. Firm in and gently water. It can help boost growth to snip the top leaves off, down to the next set of buds or foliage. Keep pots somewhere bright and warm, out of drafts.

If you wish to grow them outside in summer, be aware that these plants have been cultivated for lush quick growth, probably in a greenhouse. They are not grown as hardy garden plants like those you buy from the garden center; they are designed to be short-lived indoor plants. They will need a period of hardening off before living outdoors.

Lemongrass stalks may regenerate if put in water.

STARTED FROM STALKS

If you can find whole, intact, fresh lemongrass stalks in the store, with bases that haven't been cut off, you can try to root them to make new plants. Take three or four stalks and remove any brown old foliage, before cutting off the top third of the stalk. Pop them into a glass or jar of water and leave somewhere bright and warm indoors.

Once roots are long enough, pot up individually to grow on.

Change the water every few days. You might start to see roots forming within a week or two, but it can take a while in cooler, less bright places. Keep checking and changing the water until the roots are quite long, and the stalks look like they are about to split. Pot up each one into a container of fresh enriched potting mix and grow on until you can repot again into a larger display pot. (See *p.86 for more on lemongrass.*)

Herbs grown for the garden may be the better choice for taste and longevity.

BEST CHOICE

The varieties of herb used for supermarket produce are chosen for large yield, disease resistance, and other factors that make them ideal for agricultural production, and they may have been treated with strong chemicals to keep pests and weeds down, or to fertilize them. Cultivars bred for garden use will often be hardier and tastier, with a broader or more nuanced range of flavors. So you will get the very best herbs if you grow your own from seeds or plants intended for the home grower.

Mint may root from a supermarket bag if fresh enough.

WHY NOT TRY?

There are other fun experiments you can try to grow herbs from store-sourced produce.
- Some cut herbs, such as mint and Vietnamese coriander, may root if they are fresh enough. Snip off the bottom of the stem at an angle and place in a glass of water. Change the water as for lemongrass (see *above*).

Chamomile flowers can spring up from a tea bag's contents.

Once roots are about the length of your little finger, you can pot up into small containers of potting mix and grow on as you would any seedling.
- Split open a chamomile tea bag fresh from a sealed pack and sprinkle it onto a pot of potting mix or prepared soil in the garden, and often you will get lots of flowering plants in return.
- Dried seeds from the herb and spice aisle including dill, fennel, fenugreek,

Fenugreek is an unusual herb, so it's worth trying to raise from culinary seed.

and even coriander may germinate when you sow them if they are organic and relatively fresh. Most culinary seeds have been specially processed or heat-treated for storage and consumption, and this will prevent them from growing. However, organic seed might not have been treated this way, so the chances of sprouting success are much higher.

DIVIDING HERBS AND SAVING SEED

While it may sound as if it would be a complicated technical process, "propagation" simply refers to all the ways that you can make more plants from the ones you already have. It's an exciting thought that you can create lots of new plants, completely free. There are a number of different methods that work best for different types of herb, from annuals to evergreens. Here we will look at two of the easiest: dividing plants, and collecting and saving seed.

A large clump of oregano can be simply divided with a knife.

DIVIDING PLANTS

Deciduous perennial herbs that are more than two years old can often be propagated through division, usually in spring just as growth begins for the season. It couldn't be easier—you simply dig up a clump of the herb with a fork or spade, or pop it out of its pot. Cut through the root ball with your spade or a knife, or pull it apart with your hands, to divide it into several pieces. Each piece should have its own shoots and roots. Plant each of these new pieces further apart, in different parts of the garden or in their own pots, and water in well. Many herbs, especially those grown in containers, will benefit from being divided every few years to stop them from becoming congested and less productive.

COMING TRUE

Plants are categorized into a family, then a genus, then a species, and sometimes also a variety or cultivar. For example, dill's botanical name is *Anethum graveolens*. *Anethum* is the genus name, and *graveolens* is the species name. There are several hybrid varieties, or cultivars, of dill that also carry an extra name, such as 'Domino' and 'Fernleaf'. These have often been created through breeding to have certain characteristics, such as being slow to bolt, having leafier growth, or a better flavor.

Many of these cultivars will not "come true" from seed—this means that if you collect and sow seed from these plants, the resulting seedlings won't have all those attractive characteristics of their parent plant. Most species herbs do come true, however, so you can collect seed from them knowing they will usually be very similar to the plant you harvested them from. Plants propagated by division and by cuttings (*see pp.40–41*) match their parents exactly.

'Fernleaf' is a dill cultivar that may not come true from seed.

Fennel will produce masses of seed heads, which can be cut off and stored in paper bags to dry.

SAVING SEED

To propagate annual herbs you have to collect their seed. You can also harvest and sow the seed of biennial and some perennial herbs, too. To do this, you first have to let the herb flower, so it can set seed. Once it has finished blooming, the seed heads begin to form. Keep an eye on them—you need to catch them at the right time, just as the color begins to change. Some seed can be collected ripe and sown immediately, while others need to be almost dry when you remove them from the plant—check out details for the individual herb in the A–Z section (see pp.60–141).

When the seed heads look ready, pick a dry, calm day with no wind. For most herbs, you can simply snip off the stem and pop the seed heads whole into a paper bag. Another method that works well with large seed heads is to place the bag over the whole head, and tie it round the stem fairly tightly at the base, before cutting the stem off. This ensures you don't lose any seed.

Hang the paper bag up to dry, on a line of string with clothespins or from a clothes hanger, somewhere warm and dry with good ventilation. The seeds will drop into the bag as they dry. Alternatively, you can hang a loose bunch of stems up above a tray or place them flat on paper.

Leave for up to two weeks, then shake or scrunch the bag to release any remaining seed from the seed head, or pop them by hand out of their pod if necessary. There will often be chaff (bits of dried plant and seed casing) with the seed, and this needs to be separated out to prevent mold and disease; using a colander and a sieve can be helpful at this stage.

Place the collected seed in labeled envelopes and put them in an airtight container, such as a glass jar. This should be stored in a cool, dry place indoors until you want to sow the seeds the following spring. Check regularly for moisture, which you can reduce with a dehumidifier or by placing a small silica gel desiccant packet in each jar.

SAVE OR DIVIDE?

SAVE SEED OF: Borage • Calendula • Caraway • Chamomile • Chervil • Coriander • Dill • Fennel • Nasturtium • Parsley • Sweet cicely • Sweet marjoram

DIVIDE PLANTS OF: Basil • Catmint • Chives • Creeping thyme • Lawn chamomile • Lemongrass • Lovage • Mint • Oregano • Sorrel • Sweet woodruff • Tarragon

A sieve helps separate the seed from the chaff.

Purple basil plants can be pulled apart easily by hand.

TAKING CUTTINGS

Cuttings are pieces of a plant that have been snipped off and placed in a growing medium to root and grow on into plants. It's a thrill to see these small offcuts become whole new herbs, and at no cost to you. For some herbs that don't flower and set seed, such as lawn chamomile, this is a great way to propagate them. It's also the best method for cultivars that won't "come true" from seed (*see p.38*) but are not good candidates for division, like variegated sage. For other herbs, cuttings may be only one of several ways to propagate them, but it is often the most reliable.

PREPARING TO PROPAGATE

Before you make the cut, you need to understand a few basics to increase your chances of success, and get your tools and equipment together. Make sure your pruners or knife are sharp and sterile, and your pots or trays are clean. Also, always propagate from healthy plants—you don't want to multiply pest or disease problems in your garden.

Prepare your growing medium. It should be free-draining, but not have many nutrients, so a seed starting mix is best. Combine the seed starting mix with composted fine bark or sand to improve drainage, so the cuttings don't rot, and add perlite, which will help keep the compost moist but not wet. Ready-made cuttings mix is also available. Before inserting any cutting, dampen the soil and let any excess water drain out.

To make cuttings you need clean containers; prepared potting mix; a very sharp, clean knife or pruners; and plant material.

SUITABLE HERBS

TAKE SOFTWOOD CUTTINGS FROM: Catmint • Chamomile • Hyssop • Marjoram/oregano • Mint • Rosemary • Sage • Savory • Scented-leaf geranium • Stevia • Thyme • Wormwood

TAKE SEMI-HARDWOOD CUTTINGS FROM: Bay • Cotton lavender • Lavender • Rosemary

TAKE ROOT CUTTINGS FROM: Comfrey • Horseradish • Lemon balm • Mint • Sweet cicely • Sweet woodruff • Tarragon

Catmint (*Nepeta* spp.) grows well from softwood cuttings.

Bay (*Laurus nobilis*) is best propagated by semi-hardwood cuttings.

Mint (*Mentha* spp.) takes easily from softwood or root cuttings.

STEM CUTTINGS

There are two kinds of stem cuttings. The first of the season are softwood cuttings, usually taken from deciduous perennial herbs in spring or early summer, using the fresh new leafy growth at the tips of the plant.

Take softwood cuttings first thing in the morning—this stops them from drying out too quickly. Fill modular trays or pots with potting mix to 1 in (2 cm) of the top, firm down, and moisten.

Choose robust, nonflowering shoots. Cut them off at a sloping angle just above a pair of leaves. Place cuttings into water or a plastic bag to prevent drying out. Use the cuttings as soon as possible.

Cut off the leaves on the bottom third of the cutting, leaving the top two or three sets of leaves on the top two-thirds of the cutting. Cut off the lowest piece of stem about ¼ in (5 mm) under a node—the point from where a leaf or set of leaves sprouts. The cutting should be about 4 in (10 cm) long.

Use a dibble or pencil to poke a hole in the potting mix. Insert the cutting up to just below the lowest set of leaves, no more than 1 in (2 cm) deep. Gently firm into position. Put in a heated propagator or cover with a clear plastic bag and secure with a rubber band, being careful not to let the bag touch the leaves. Take the bag off every few days, or turn inside out, to remove condensed moisture. Place the propagator or bagged pot somewhere warm and bright but out of direct sunlight.

Roots should appear at the bottom of the pot or tray within a month, but it can vary depending on the herb. Leave them for another two weeks or so before potting up individually into fresh potting mix in small containers. Just like seedlings, rooted cuttings need to be hardened off before being moved outside to develop further. Half-hardy and tender herbs, such as scented-leaf geranium, may have to stay under cover until all risk of frost has passed in the following spring before going outside.

Semi-hardwood or semi-ripe stem cuttings are usually used for evergreen plants and are taken in summer or early fall. The process is the same as for softwood cuttings, but instead of putting in a heated propagator or bag, place pots under cover in a cool place such as an unheated greenhouse or conservatory or cold frame. You should see roots forming at the bottom of the pots or tray in 1–2 months.

Cut the stem just under a node, the point where a set of leaves were.

At your worktop, cut off the lower leaves of the cutting.

Insert the cutting 1 in (2 cm) deep in pots or tray modules.

ROOT CUTTINGS

For root cuttings, a section of root is cut off and planted up to produce a new plant. This can be done in spring or fall. If the herbs are pot-grown, simply pop them out of the pot and snip off a length of healthy root with visible buds on it, about 2 in (5 cm) long. Dig up or dig around plants in the ground to expose the roots, and then cut. Some herbs, like horseradish, regenerate from any small piece of root, so you can slice it into several pieces and plant each one.

Use a dibble or pencil to make a hole in the potting mix before inserting the root cutting into the tray or pot. Cover it with potting mix and firm in. Top with gravel and label the pot or tray, so you remember which plant you are rooting. Place in a sheltered or covered area outside, such as in a cold frame.

It takes about three weeks for cuttings to root and start to put on top growth. Do not water in this period. Then, if it is springtime, water and feed them, and harden them off once all risk of frost has passed. If it is fall, keep them in the cold frame over winter, and then do as for spring, before potting on or planting out.

Use pruners to cut the root into sections after digging the plant up.

TROUBLESHOOTING

Herbs are generally untroubled by garden pests and diseases, but there are a few to consider, and some common problems. Many can be easily avoided with good cultivation practices including having the best soil, drainage, and light for the plant, preparing the ground well, and watering the right amount.

APHIDS

PROBLEM Stunted and distorted growth, brown patches, and spread of viruses on a broad range of plants.
CAUSE Green, brown, or black sap-sucking insects, which puncture leaves to feed on sap.
REMEDY Rub off by hand, or wash off with horticultural soap. Attract aphid predators (ladybugs and hoverflies).

BOLTING

PROBLEM Plants like coriander and dill send up flower shoots too fast, with few leaves produced.
CAUSE Dry or poor soil, hot weather, not enough space.
REMEDY Sow herbs at the right time and succession sow regularly for those prone to bolting. Keep herbs well watered and give them room to grow.

SLUGS & SNAILS

PROBLEM Holes in leaves or foliage and flowers disappearing.
CAUSE Slugs and snails feeding on plants, especially at night or in wet weather.
REMEDY Clear debris where they hide. Seek out and remove by hand. Cover soil with gravel or eggshells. Try copper strips around pot rims, and beer traps and slug pellets on the ground.

CATERPILLARS

PROBLEM Patches of foliage eaten during spring and summer.
CAUSE Caterpillars of butterflies and moths feeding on leaves.
REMEDY Pick off by hand when seen or seek out at night. However, many caterpillars that eat herbs become beneficial butterflies, so leave them be where possible.

FLEA BEETLE

PROBLEM Lots of small holes in the foliage of leafy herbs such as arugula.
CAUSE Tiny jumping black beetles feeding on the leaves.
REMEDY Establish seedlings and young plants quickly with regular watering. Clean up debris in the fall. Organic contact insecticides for edible plants are also available.

RUST

PROBLEM Herbs, particularly mint, oregano, and savory, produce distorted growth covered in orange powder and drop leaves.
CAUSE A fungal disease.
REMEDY Immediately remove whole infected plants. Don't plant affected herbs in that area again, and don't put infected plants on the compost heap.

GRAY MOLD

PROBLEM Gray fuzzy growth on foliage and flowers, which then turn brown and collapse.
CAUSE A fungal disease.
REMEDY Avoid overcrowding plants, maintain air movement, and ventilate indoor growing areas. Remove dead and dying material and destroy immediately. Do not compost.

LEAFHOPPER

PROBLEM Rough, pale mottling on mint, sage, rosemary, oregano, catmint, and lavender.
CAUSE Small white sap-sucking hopping insects, which are often found on the underside of leaves.
REMEDY Affected plants are safe to eat, and if the damage is not extensive, these pests can mostly be tolerated.

DAMPING OFF

PROBLEM Seedlings sown indoors develop fluffy fungus and flop.
CAUSE Fungal diseases.
REMEDY Keep all tools and pots clean and sow into fresh, clean seed starting mix. Make sure there is good air circulation. Avoid overcrowding seedlings, keep them well ventilated to reduce humidity, and don't overwater.

POWDERY MILDEW

PROBLEM Dusty white film on the foliage of herbs, which may turn black
CAUSE A fungal disease.
REMEDY Infection is more common in dry conditions, so water regularly and maintain good air circulation. Clean up infected debris from around plants. Organic fungicides are available. Do not compost infected plants.

Cooking with herbs is enjoyable at any age. Adding a mixture of herbs to a basic muffin recipe is easy and fun to do, with delicious results.

USING HERBS

Herbs are, essentially, useful plants—those whose leaves, seeds, or flowers are valued for their flavor, perfume, or medicinal qualities. These remarkable plants soothe us with their scents, and make a delicious difference to food and drinks by adding incomparable, fresh flavors to savory and sweet dishes and beverages. In this section, find out how to harvest and store fresh herbs so they are at their best and last as long as possible. Discover different ways to use them in the kitchen and home, and learn how to dry and preserve them to use later.

HARVESTING HERBS

Some herbs, such as dill, chervil, and cilantro, may be ready for picking from as soon as 6–8 weeks after sowing, while others, such as basil, may not be ready until at least 1–2 months after planting out. The most important thing to remember is to harvest often, because the more you pick from a herb plant, the more robust and vigorous it will become.

Pick herbs regularly and often for strong growth and the freshest leaves.

HOW TO HARVEST

As a general rule, for annuals and biennials grown from seed, and for established perennial herbs that resprout each spring, it is safe to commence harvesting leaves once the plants have developed 4–8 or more sets of leaves, or once they have grown more than 4 in (10 cm) tall.

Herb leaves tend to have the best flavor before the plant flowers, and you should only harvest nonflowering stems. Flowering deciduous perennial herbs can be cut back and fed to encourage a fresh flush of leaves. Discard annual herbs that have already bolted or flowered.

Pick leaves in the morning, before the aromatic oils dissipate in the sunshine, or when it is overcast. Make sure you snip off stems or stalks right down to their base, rather than picking single leaves and leaving a dead-ended stalk behind. Use sharp scissors or pruners, and harvest from the outside of the plant and, with branching herbs, from the top, cutting down the tips, which are the freshest growth. Don't use any leaves or stems that look damaged or affected by pests or diseases.

Chives should be harvested by cutting right back to the base of the plant.

Even if you just want to use the leaves, you should harvest parsley by cutting the whole stalk.

PERFECT PICKING

Annual herbs can usually be picked a little all season long, or cut back completely about twice in a season. If you are only growing one plant of a particular herb, don't take more than a third of it at one time. If you have several plants, clip them in rotation. Harvest one down to about 6 in (15 cm) from the base, and then feed with general purpose fertilizer. While it regenerates with fresh growth, which should take several weeks, you can harvest from the other plants. You should make your final harvest of annuals as the weather cools in early fall. The plants can then be lifted and discarded on the compost heap.

Perennials take a little longer to establish, so pick only small amounts or cut back the whole plant just once during its first growing season. In subsequent years, you might get 2–3 harvests. Follow the same pattern as with annuals—harvest down to about 6 in (15 cm) from the base of the plant, and then feed. Make your last harvest of deciduous herbs in late summer.

With evergreens such as thyme and rosemary, never cut into the woody growth toward the base, and don't cut back the whole plant or pick too much after the first frost—you can keep picking sparingly through winter, but be aware that the plants will not actively put on fresh growth again until spring.

To harvest flowers, pick blooms as they open for maximum freshness. For seeds (see p.39), harvesting for the kitchen is the same process as collecting seed for sowing later. Roots can be harvested after one or two full seasons of growth, usually in the fall. Look at the A–Z section (see pp.60–141) for details for each plant. Dig around the plant before lifting it out of the soil with a fork, gently. Cut off the stems and leaves and any fibrous roots before washing off the soil and patting the root dry.

Sage and mint produce leaves prolifically that can be picked all season.

STORING FRESH

You should always use your harvested herbs as soon as possible after picking, but if you can't, they can still be kept fresh for a few days. Don't wash them; the water will degrade their quality more quickly. Some herbs, such as basil and cilantro, do best when placed as a bunch of stems in a jar or glass of cold water, like a flower bouquet. Basil prefers to stay at room temperature, while cilantro can go in the fridge— some recommend putting a clear plastic bag over the top. Refrigerating will keep leaves fresh for 3–7 days. Change the water every few days.

For leafy herbs such as sorrel and arugula, or sprigs of rosemary and thyme, you can put them in a sealed food storage bag with most of the air pressed out, and place in the salad crisper drawer of the fridge. Moisture-loving herbs like mint will benefit from being wrapped in a barely damp sheet of paper towel in the bag.

You can also try an herb keeper. These usually have compartments for different types of herbs and a water reservoir, and fit neatly in your fridge door.

To store herbs in the longer term, you can dry them (see p.56) or freeze or preserve them (see p.54).

An herb keeper is a handy gadget for helping cut herbs stay fresh.

For supermarket cut herbs, store them as you would homegrown ones.

BOUGHT CUT HERBS

The advice for how to store freshly picked herbs also applies to cut herbs bought from the supermarket. Always buy cut herbs as close to your cooking time as possible, and choose those that look healthy—avoid blackened or yellowing, soggy clumps. When you get home, take them out of any packaging and remove any ties or rubber bands. Snip off the bottom of the stems, and then treat them like picked herbs.

CULINARY HERBS

Herbs can elevate any recipe you make to a higher level, adding pep and brightness to the dullest dinner and making even a simple salad taste so much more delicious. Some herbs are best used at the start of cooking; others are better added at the end or used fresh. Either way, they are an invaluable tool in the kitchen, adding depth of flavor in the cooking pot or zest and freshness as a garnish.

Keep freshly picked herbs on hand so you can use them quickly.

Cilantro is best added at the end of cooking or as a garnish.

ADDING LAST MINUTE

Soft leafy herbs, such as basil, cilantro, and parsley, can lose flavor when cooked too long and are generally best used fresh in salads and salad dressings, to garnish hot or cold dishes, or added at the very end of cooking. Chopping them up, or tearing larger leaves such as basil with your hands, releases the herb's oils, so when you stir it in or sprinkle over your dish before serving, it will impart the best taste and aroma. Always chop or tear your fresh, leafy herbs just before you use them, as they quickly lose their vibrancy if left to sit.

Herbs can make the whole dish, as when arugula leaves are used as a salad, with herb flowers and an herby vinaigrette.

EASY CHOPPING

When you are chopping herbs, whether using a knife, scissors, a food processor, or a blender, make sure the blades are sharp. This will ensure that the leaves will be cut rather than crushed, which can turn them black around the edges and mar the flavor.

If you regularly need to chop large quantities of herbs, consider using herb scissors, which have five blades to help you cut quickly and evenly. You can also use a mezzaluna or hachoir herb chopper, with a curved blade and two handles. You rock it back and forth across the herbs and it makes light work of chopping a bunch of stems and leaves. Sometimes these blades come with a board that has a curved indentation in the middle to make it even easier to use, but any cutting board will do.

You need a well-sharpened knife to chop parsley very finely.

A mezzaluna is often the best tool to use when chopping a quantity of herbs.

TOP TIP FOR BROAD-LEAVED HERBS, LIKE SORREL, TRY THE CHIFFONADE TECHNIQUE TO MAKE DELICATE RIBBONS OR SHREDS. STACK THE LEAVES ON TOP OF EACH OTHER, ROLL THEM UP TIGHTLY INTO A CIGAR SHAPE, AND CUT ACROSS THEM THINLY ALL THE WAY ALONG. YOU CAN ALSO DO THIS WITH BASIL LEAVES INSTEAD OF TEARING THEM.

BRILLIANT BOUQUETS

When using several different woody herbs in a dish, fishing out individual leaves from a pot before serving can be challenging, and sometimes sprigs of herbs such as rosemary or thyme will break apart during cooking. To keep them together and make removal as easy as possible, you can use a bundle or sachet of mixed herbs tied up together; this is often known as a *bouquet garni*. A traditional *bouquet garni* contains parsley, thyme, and a bay leaf—though other herbs are sometimes added—and is either tied in a bunch with kitchen string, or wrapped up in a piece of cheesecloth.

Other classic herb mixtures include *fines herbes*, which is usually made with fresh parsley, chives, chervil, and tarragon; and *herbes de Provence*, which is a variable mix of dried herbs such as rosemary, marjoram, thyme, and savory. You could also group together oregano, basil, thyme, sage, and rosemary for an Italian-inspired herb bouquet.

Tie together a bay leaf, parsley, and thyme to make a classic *bouquet garni*.

You can add a bay leaf to infuse milk at the start of cooking a white sauce.

IN THE POT

Woody herbs, such as rosemary, thyme, sage, and bay, are tougher than fresh soft leafy herbs and generally are not eaten raw, as they are often too powerful to be palatable and have a less attractive mouthfeel. They are ideal for using throughout the cooking process to draw out lots of flavor in stews, soups, casseroles, stocks, roasts, and sauces. Add whole leaves or sprigs right from the beginning of cooking.

SWEET AND FRUITY HERBS

We mainly think of herbs as flavor enhancers for savory food, but they can contribute so much to sweet cakes, cookies, desserts, and drinks from cordials to tea. You can infuse fruity herbs, like lemon verbena, in milk or cream to flavor set and chilled desserts, add pineapple sage leaves to a tropical fruit salad or punch, pair basil with strawberries, or mix mint into chocolate mousse.

A tropical fruit punch is enlivened by sprigs of fresh mint.

Stevia leaves are a natural sweetener many times stronger than sugar.

BRILLIANT BAKING

When it comes to baking, herbs can bring subtle flavor notes and reduce the amount of sugar you need to use. With dried and ground stevia leaves, for example, one teaspoon can be equal in sweetness to up to 10 teaspoons of sugar. The intensity of the sweetness and flavor very much depends on the individual plant and your growing conditions, including how much light it

Use rosemary to flavor and decorate a juicy olive oil and polenta cake.

gets, so there are no hard and fast rules, and it's best to experiment and see what suits your palate. Sweet cicely has a similar characteristic, in that you can use it to take the tart edge off fruit in cooking, meaning you don't need to use as much sugar for pie and tart fillings, fools, and compotes.

Many savory herbs can also be used in sweet baking in order to add an extra dimension in recipes such as rosemary and polenta cake.

SUGAR INFUSION

Lavender adds a lovely scent and flavor to treats like shortbread or cakes, but it's difficult to gauge the right amount to use, as too much can end up tasting overpowering and soapy. Instead, impart just the right hint of lavender by infusing your baking sugar with its flowers about a week before you use it. Cut the flower stems when in bud, just before they open, and strip from the stalk. Use a tablespoon of lavender florets to every cup of sugar. Place in a jar with a lid for a week, and sift out the flowers before adding to the dough—unless you want a stronger flavor and those tell-tale purple flecks throughout. You can also try this method with whole leaf sprigs of other herbs, like lemon thyme.

Lavender sugar adds a fragrant note to lemon and lavender bars.

SUPER SYRUP

Enjoy more interesting herb flavors in lots of exciting ways by infusing them into a sugar syrup. This versatile liquid can then be used to sweeten summer drinks like lemonade, or to make iced delights such as granitas and sorbets. A splash will lend some zing to cake icing, or you can drizzle the raw syrup over sponge cake or ice cream as a topping. You can even add a dash to liven up your morning coffee. A general rule for a simple syrup is to use one part water to one part sugar, and add in as much or as little herb as you wish—a few sprigs or leaves can be enough.

One very special beverage that you can make from an infused syrup at home, but will never find in stores, is a rose-scented geranium cordial, using the leaves of a cultivar such as *Pelargonium* 'Attar of Roses'. Heat up 3½ cups (1 liter) of water in a saucepan with 10 cups (2 kg) of superfine sugar and a bunch of rose-scented geranium leaves, stirring occasionally, until all the sugar is dissolved. When cool, remove the leaves. Add to cocktails or, to turn the syrup into cordial, add the juice of 6 lemons and the zest of 2. Store in a sterilized jar or bottle for up to 3–4 days in the fridge. Add sparkling water to make a refreshing drink.

***Pelargonium* 'Attar of Roses'** has the most intensely rose-scented leaves.

TEA TIME

We often call a hot drink made with herbs an herbal "tea," but in fact the correct term is a tisane—an infusion made from the leaves, flowers, roots, or seeds. When you grow your own herbs it's easy to make a variety of fresh and soothing herbal drinks whenever you please. The most common herbs for tisanes are mint, chamomile, lemon verbena, ginger, and lemongrass.

Making a tisane is much like making normal tea. However, with a teabag, you might just dunk it in the water for a few moments and go, and with tea leaves in a pot you would not normally let them stew for more than 4–5 minutes, but when making your own herbal tea with fresh herbs, it can take up to 15 minutes to develop the flavor, depending on how strong you like it. You may have to try tasting the tisane a few times until you find your preferred steeping time. Make

sure the pot has a well-fitting lid to prevent essential oils from evaporating. You may wish to cover your pot with a tea cozy to keep it warm while it infuses. You can also make your tisane in a tisaniere; these are typically designed with a central chamber to house the herbs, so you don't need a strainer when pouring the tea out.

In summer, let the infusion cool and pour over ice with a slice of lemon to make a cooling, nonalcoholic sundowner.

Place your fresh herbs in a teapot and cover with boiling water.

Place the lid on firmly and leave to infuse for your preferred time.

When ready, pour out into a cup using a tea-strainer to catch any stray leaves.

EDIBLE BLOOMS

Herbs can offer more than leaves, seeds, and roots, bringing beautiful blooms of vibrant color and welcome form to the garden. Most herb flowers are also edible—in fact, many people grow herbs like borage and nasturtiums specifically for their blooms. As well as edible flowers grown from deliberately planted herbs, you can find them for free in the wild and weedy patches of your yard and local hedgerows.

FLOWER POWER

Herb flowers are used in many ways. Some, such as nasturtiums, add a peppery kick to leaf salads. Calendula petals are a perfect replacement for saffron or turmeric to add color to rice dishes, and cornflowers and chamomile make soothing herbal tea. Borage blooms make a pretty garnish for drinks as well as adding a cucumber tang. The leaves of herbs are often less palatable after they have flowered, but the flowers themselves can then be harvested to eat—try breaking up chive flowers and adding them to everything from couscous to pasta sauces.

Crystallized or candied violets are easy to make. All you need is an egg white and a few tablespoons of superfine sugar.

Nasturtiums, calendula, and borage are favorite edible herb flowers.

GREAT FOR BAKING

Sweet violets make dainty decoration for cakes, cupcakes, desserts, and ice cream. They can be used plain and fresh, or preserved and sweetened by crystallizing or candying them. Keep at least 1 in (2 cm) of stem attached to the flowers so they are easy to work with. You can simply paint them with egg white and dip them in superfine sugar or, for a fluffier version, whisk up the egg white, dip each flower in it, place them on a plate and sprinkle or sift with the sugar, and then place on a piece of paper towel or parchment paper. Pop the blooms in the fridge overnight and then keep at room temperature for most of the next day to dry. Remove the stems and store the glazed blooms in an airtight container until you need them. Use within a month.

GO WILD

Some plants we think of as weeds, such as dandelions, are actually valuable edible herbs that are packed with nutrients and available for free from your lawn or neglected nooks and crannies of the garden. You can eat the flowers as well as the leaves of many of these much-maligned but often magnificent plants.

Outside of the garden, you may also find tasty wild plants such as salad burnet and elderflower. One of the tastiest edible floral treats you can make in late spring and early summer are elderflower fritters. Gather the blossoms in the morning as they open— try to collect away from the pollution of busy roads. Mix ¾ cup (100g) of self-rising flour with 2 teaspoons of cornstarch and 2 teaspoons of superfine sugar. Add one beaten egg and then slowly whisk in ½ cup (150ml) of sparkling water. Dip the flower heads in the batter and deep fry until lightly golden. Dust with powdered sugar or drizzle honey over, and enjoy. Dandelion flower heads can be cooked in the same way, with a slightly crunchier result.

Dandelion flower petals are used to make dandelion wine, and can be added to salads, pancakes, omelets, and risottos.

Elderflower fritters are a sweet delicacy best made when the flower buds are freshly open.

PRESERVING HERBS

Sometimes you may find yourself with a glut of one herb or another in the garden, and though you want to use it all fresh, it's just not possible. Or you may have a leftover bunch of herbs that is about to start wilting. You can prevent food waste and use herbs in lots of delicious dishes later on by preserving them in oil or freezing them. These methods allow you to enjoy the flavor of fresh herbs all year, and are ideal for herbs that don't dry well.

Steeping herbs in vinegar or oil is a good way to preserve their flavor.

FREEZING HERBS

Freezing is the best way to store herbs long-term while retaining the best flavor and the most nutritional value. Using ice-cube trays gives you handy, small portions suitable for most recipes.

First, take the leaves off the stems and chop them finely using a sharp knife, or in a food processor with a little oil. Spoon portions of the chopped herb into an ice-cube tray, and add oil to each cube, making sure there is a thin layer of oil on top of the herbs (you may have added enough oil in the food processor). Place in the freezer. Once the cubes have frozen, pop them into a food storage freezer bag. Push most of the air out of the bag before sealing, label it with the name of the herb and the date, and put it in the freezer.

Frozen herbs become slightly mushy, so they are good for using in hot dishes like sauces, stews, casseroles, and soups, but not as a garnish, or in salads. When making a hot dish you don't have to defrost the cubes—just add them straight into whatever you are cooking, in the same amount that you would fresh. The little amount of oil in the cube won't dilute the consistency of the dish.

Frozen ice cubes of herbs make convenient portions that can be quickly added to cooking when needed.

Although it may be easier to use herbs frozen in oil for cooking, you can also simply freeze chopped herbs in water instead. Make sure the herbs are wholly submerged in the water before freezing.

TOP HERBS FOR FREEZING
Basil • Borage • Chives • Dill • Fennel • Mint • Oregano • Parsley • Sage • Savory • Sorrel • Tarragon • Thyme

TOP TIP TO MAKE PRETTY AND TASTY ICE CUBES FOR DRINKS, FREEZE HERB FLOWER HEADS AND WHOLE, UNCUT LEAVES IN ICE-CUBE TRAYS.

You can make herb oil with a pestle and mortar as you would a pesto, adding much more oil. Used fresh, it will be safe and delicious.

HERB OILS

Make quick salad dressings and pesto-style sauces by blending up your favorite fresh leaves with olive, sunflower, or rapeseed oil. These will keep happily in the fridge for a few days, and bring real zing to any meal.

However, infusing fresh herbs in oil long-term is a different matter. There are countless recipes and instructions available in cookbooks and online, which direct you to place fresh herbs like basil or rosemary, and even vegetables like garlic and chiles, into bottles of oil to use in the kitchen. Some recommend blanching the herbs first or heating up the oil with the herbs in it first. Many people are unaware that none of these methods can be considered truly safe for the home cook.

The bottles of infused oil that you find for sale in stores have been through an industrial factory process of acidification to make them safe to consume (but it is still best to keep them in the fridge and use them within a few weeks once open). If you make your own at home, or are given homemade infused oils as gifts, they may be contaminated with botulism—a serious, possibly fatal toxin that is odorless and tasteless, which develops when spores grow on the fresh material in the oil over time in the absence of oxygen.

It's best to stick to either freshly made herb oil, which you can store for a day or two in the fridge, or frozen herb oil cubes (see *opposite*). It is not advised to push sprigs of fresh herbs into bottles of oil, leave them on the kitchen counter, and use them for months.

HERB-INFUSED EXTRAS

Two safe and appetizing ways to impart more herb flavor into your food are with infused salt or vinegar. The vinegar can be used in salad dressings, sauces, and marinades, while herb salt can be used just like normal salt when cooking, but has an extra kick of flavor.

Mix chopped herbs up with sea salt, or pound them together in a pestle and mortar, in a ratio of one-third herb to two-thirds salt. Spread the mixture out on a tray or plate to dry for 24 hours, before storing it in a jar or airtight container. It will keep fresh for several weeks. You can make celery salt with the seeds of leaf celery, or you could try making dill salt, a classic ingredient for gravlax, and you will also get very good results with lemon thyme, rosemary, and mint.

To make herb-infused vinegar, add lightly crushed herbs to a jar or bottle of vinegar and allow it to steep at room temperature for a couple of weeks, out of direct sunlight. Store in a clean glass bottle with a lid. It will keep on the kitchen counter for a month or so, and three months or longer in the fridge.

Parsley herb salt makes a colorful and tasty condiment.

DRYING HERBS

Dried herbs can be the best choice when the recipe calls for a long cook, or to use over winter when fresh harvests are minimal. Drying gets rid of the water in a leaf while keeping the important aromatic oils that give flavor and fragrance. It preserves the taste of the herb, and sometimes concentrates it, too, and drying your own at home means you are assured of the highest quality. Herbs such as bay, lavender, mint, lemon balm, thyme, and rosemary dry very well, while softer herbs like tarragon and chives are better frozen to preserve them (see p.54).

Cover a baking rack with tightly stretched cheesecloth and place herb leaves carefully on top, spread out in one layer.

Bunches of herbs can be hung upside down from a line to dry in an area with good ventilation.

AIR-DRYING

Air-drying herbs is easy, particularly for those with broader foliage, such as mint, bay, and sage, but it is suitable for all but the softest of herbs. First, decide where you are going to dry them: you will need an airy, dry, dark, and relatively warm space. An airing cupboard, if you have one, would be ideal. Many people use a spare room with the curtains or blinds pulled (to make it dark) and the door left open (for airflow), or an attic, provided that the space is not cold.

Drying on a rack takes up a lot of surface space but is the quickest method, and so there is less chance of mold developing. There are special herb-drying racks available with wooden slats or mesh panels, but you can also use cooling racks for baking with a piece of cheesecloth on top. Take leaves off their stems and spread them out in a single layer. Place in the drying area, and turn the leaves or sprigs twice a day for three days. You will know they are done when they crumble when handled.

An alternative way to air-dry herbs is to hang them in bunches. Bind about 10 stems together loosely with string, and hang them upside down in the drying area. This way of drying can take up to two weeks.

Herb leaves for oven-drying should be stripped from their stems.

OVEN-DRYING HERBS

The most straightforward method of drying herbs is to use a food dehydrator. If you don't have one, you can replicate the same process by drying them in your oven, set low. However, it can take some trial and error to find the best technique and timing for you. This method works best for tougher herbs, such as sage, rosemary, and thyme.

Strip the leaves off the stems, and spread them out in a single layer on a rack covered in cheesecloth, or on a baking sheet covered in parchment paper with some holes punched into it. Turn the oven onto its lowest possible setting and pop in the rack or tray.

A food dehydrator will dry herbs quickly and easily.

Check the herbs regularly to make sure they are not burned, and turn them over or stir them gently after half an hour. After an hour, turn off the oven but leave them inside until it cools.

MICROWAVE MAGIC

The quickest method of all involves drying herbs in the microwave. The water is eliminated in moments, leaving the leaves green and looking fresh. However, it can be tricky to get it right; a couple of seconds can make the difference between spot-on and singed. To try it out, take the herb leaves off the stems and spread them out between two layers of paper towel on a microwave-safe plate. Turn on full for 1 minute, and check. Keep adding 20 or 30 seconds then checking until they crumble. Watch out—they burn easily.

Bay and other herbs can be dried in a microwave between sheets of paper towel.

Herbs must be completely dry before being placed in a container to store.

STORING DRIED HERBS

Once dried, crumble the herbs between your fingers or in a mortar and pestle. Remove any pieces of stalk. Some herbs, like bay leaves, can be left whole. Put the dried herbs in small airtight containers, such as glass jars with a screw-on lid,

Clip- and screw-top jars are good containers for home-dried herbs .

and store them in a cupboard or somewhere else out of the light. For the first month, check the jar regularly to see if moisture has been trapped inside—if so, the herbs are not fully dry and should be taken out and redried before storing again. They should keep their flavor for up to a year.

> **TOP TIP** DRIED HERBS CAN BE MUCH STRONGER IN FLAVOR THAN FRESH HERBS. WHEN A RECIPE CALLS FOR A CERTAIN AMOUNT OF FRESH HERB, SUBSTITUTE A THIRD OF THAT AMOUNT OF DRIED—FOR EXAMPLE, A TABLESPOON OF FRESH HERB SHOULD BE REPLACED WITH A TEASPOON OF DRIED.

HERBS FOR FRAGRANCE

Some of the best attributes of herbs are their aromas, which can evoke everything from a tasty Sunday roast dinner to memories of childhood holidays. Brushing past an herb bush in the garden will release a wonderful whiff of heady fragrance that can be an energizing experience, or sometimes a relaxing one. When you grow your own herbs, you can easily translate these mood-enhancing qualities into your everyday activities at home.

Protect your woolens with sachets of strong-smelling insect-repellent herbs, such as wormwood and feverfew.

SWELL SMELLS

One of the best ways to take advantage of herbs' sensational scents is to make sachets of dried, fragrant herbs. You can make a simple pouch with some muslin and ribbon, or put your sewing skills to the test with leftover scraps of fabric. These herbs will keep your clothes drawer smelling fresh and fragrant, and sachets made from herbs including wormwood, cotton lavender, and feverfew are also used to keep unwanted insects such as clothes moths from damaging the precious items in your wardrobe.

Another excellent use for your favorite aromatic herbs is to infuse them in water, and then pour the liquid into a pump bottle. This scented spray can then be used when ironing laundry, or to give a room or bedding a quick, sweet-smelling spritz.

FAVORITE HERBS FOR SCENT

Bee balm • Catmint • Chamomile • Cotton lavender • Hyssop • Lavender • Lemon thyme • Lemon verbena • Mint • Pineapple sage • Rosemary • Savory • Scented-leaf geranium • Sweet woodruff • Wormwood

Sachets filled with sweet-scented herbs like lemon thyme or sweet woodruff will perfume your drawers and cupboards.

Use a pump bottle filled with water infused with herbs such as rosemary or lavender as a room or laundry spray.

> **TOP TIP** PLANT HERBS THAT YOU ARE GROWING SPECIFICALLY TO USE FOR FRAGRANCE IN FULL SUN TO BOOST THE AROMATIC OILS IN THE LEAVES, AND PLACE THEM NEAR SEATING AREAS OUTSIDE, SO YOU CAN EASILY REACH OUT AND RUB THE LEAVES TO RELEASE THOSE PLEASING SCENTS INTO THE AIR.

BLISSFUL BATHS

Pamper yourself with an aromatherapy bath scented with garden herbs. Simply tie a bunch of stems together and drop them in the bath as the water runs, or fill a mesh bag with herbs and immerse it in the water or hang it from the hot tap so the water runs through the herbs.

Alternatively, try making your own bath bombs. Mix ½ cup (100g) baking soda, ¼ cup (50g) citric acid, 3 tbsp (25g) cornstarch, and 3 tbsp (25g) Epsom salts in a large bowl. Add your chosen scented dried herb leaves, flowers, or decorative petals. Slowly whisk in 2 tablespoons of olive, coconut, rapeseed, or sunflower oil. Add a few squirts or drops of water

and pull the mix together with your hands. Pack it very firmly into molds—these can be anything from repurposed muffin tins to ones made specifically for bath bombs. Leave them to dry out for a few hours before using.

If you want brightly colored bombs, add a few drops of liquid food coloring with the oil at the start.

Mix your herbs and other ingredients in a bowl and then add a squirt of water.

Press the mixture together with your hands to firm it up.

Pack the mixture tightly into your chosen molds and then leave to dry.

POTPOURRI

Forget plug-in air fresheners, aerosol sprays, and scented candles—with homegrown herbs you can have your own fabulous room scent, just how you like it, with a bowl of homemade potpourri. Dried herbs and flowers can impart a soft, light, natural background scent, rather than the over-strong smell of commercial types, which are often made with added dyes and concentrated essential oils. Pick herb scents that work together, and think about texture and color, too, by using the flowers and petals of herbs like hops, marigolds, and cornflowers. If you want to keep your mix smelling fresh longer, you can add a fixative such as orris root powder, which comes from irises.

Use lots of different dried herb leaves and flower petals with spices and fruit to make your own potpourri.

Herbs have a variety of leaf shapes and foliage color, so grouping them together is an attractive way of growing them. This herb garden combines thyme, lavender, and rosemary plants to make the most of their decorative appeal.

HERBS A–Z

There are lots of different herbs available, with a wide range of exciting flavors, scents, and applications. Our A–Z guide features detailed profiles of some of the most popular and beneficial garden herbs. It will help you understand, quickly and easily, how and where you can cultivate each one in your garden, as well as providing useful tips on harvesting and using these herbs in the kitchen and home. There is also information on propagation and, where relevant, the top cultivars to grow for best results.

CHIVES *ALLIUM*

The hollow, grasslike leaves of this perennial have a pungent scent and mild oniony flavor, and are topped with a swath of edible purple-mauve globe-shaped flowers in summer. Among the first herbs to emerge each season, chives grow vigorously and can be cut repeatedly for a continual supply.

PLANT TYPE Semi-evergreen perennial
HARDINESS Hardy
HEIGHT Up to 16 in (40 cm)
SPREAD 10 in (25 cm)
SOIL Any moist, well-drained soil
LIGHT ☼ ☽

Chives are easy to grow and are particularly attractive in flower, so they make an ideal starter plant for any herb garden.

GROW AND MAINTAIN

The two most widely grown chives are the common chive (*Allium schoenoprasum*), and the garlic chive (*A. tuberosum*). Common chives have slender tubular leaves and pretty, globular flowers in shades of purple through to pink, and grow to about 12 in (30 cm). Garlic chives are taller, with white flowers and flatter leaves, and have a more garlicky taste and aroma. Both can be grown from seed and harvested in their first season. *A. schoenoprasum* has two excellent cultivars for flowers: 'Black Isle Blush', with light mauve blooms with a deep pink center, and 'Forescate', which has larger, pink flowers.

Chives need warmth to germinate. Sow seeds indoors in early spring, and keep in a heated propagator to give them

Plant chives in a row to make a decorative edging to a bed or path.

Garlic chives are much used in Chinese and East Asian cuisine.

Gently pull apart a congested clump of chives and replant them separately.

PROPAGATE As a bulbous plant, chives multiply and get congested over the years. Lift and divide the bulbs into smaller clumps and replant them every two to three years, in spring or fall.

HARVEST

Chives can be harvested throughout the growing season. Let plants grown from seed establish until midsummer in their first year before cutting. Snip off as much as you need with scissors, about 1 in (3 cm) from the base, working from the outside in. New leaves will grow back quickly. If growing for leaves, remove the flower stems as they appear. Cut the whole plant back to about 2 in (5 cm) from the base in midsummer to encourage new leaves. Grow separate plants for a harvest of flowers. After flowering, cut the whole plant back to the base.

a start before planting out in late spring. Alternatively, sow seeds directly into the soil in late spring. You can also buy pot-grown plants. Plant out in an open position in rich, moist but well-drained soil in full sun or part-shade, spaced 6 in (15 cm) apart. If planting chives to make an attractive edging along a path, space plants 4 in (10 cm) apart. Water regularly, and apply a liquid feed in

spring. In milder climates they may even grow through winter, but if plants die back, they will regrow in spring.

Chives also do well in containers, but may be more prone to aphids in pots. Watch out, too, for rust and powdery mildew (see pp.42–43). In both cases, cutting back all growth should save the plant, but be sure to destroy rather than compost the clippings.

USES

Chives are predominantly a culinary herb used as a garnish and flavoring for dips, such as sour cream and chive, for soups such as mushroom or potato and leek, and especially for egg dishes such as omelets and egg salad. Add after cooking for the best flavor. Cut chives will last up to a week in a food storage bag in the fridge. They don't dry well but can be preserved in ice cubes for later use. The flowers, broken up, add color and flavor to salads.

A few chopped chives are all you need to impart an oniony tang.

Harvests of leaves are quickly replaced with new growth.

LEMON VERBENA

ALOYSIA CITRODORA

This woody perennial produces upright stems of lance-shaped leaves that have a strong, citrusy fragrance and taste—fresh and sweet with a zesty kick like lemon candies. In mid- to late summer, it is topped with delicate sprays of tiny white to pale pink or lilac flowers that help attract pollinators.

PLANT TYPE Deciduous subshrub
HARDINESS Half-hardy
HEIGHT Up to 8 ft (2.5 m)
SPREAD Up to 8 ft (2.5 m)
SOIL Any soil except clay
LIGHT ☀

Grow lemon verbena near seating areas to ward off unwanted insects.

GROW AND MAINTAIN

Originally from South America, lemon verbena loves warm, humid conditions, and is hardy only in mild or coastal areas. Elsewhere, it needs winter protection from frost, wind, and temperatures below 40°F (4°C).

Sowing seed is rarely successful in cooler climates, so buy plants to grow instead. Plant in well-drained soil in a warm, sheltered situation, such as at the base of a sunny, south-facing wall. If planting several, set them 3 ft (1 m) apart. Mulch with compost or organic material in the fall to protect the roots.

Alternatively, grow in a container that can be moved to a frost-free location over winter. Use a pot at least 8–12 in (20–30 cm) in diameter and plant in an enriched potting mix. Once all risk of frost has passed, place the container outside in a warm, sunny spot. Water throughout the growing season, and feed with liquid fertilizer when it is flowering. In the fall, move to a cool spot indoors; even here, it will drop all leaves in winter. Plants that have overwintered outdoors may regenerate from the base quite late in the following season, so have patience.

PROPAGATE Take softwood cuttings from new growth in late spring. You can also take semi-hardwood cuttings in late summer or early fall. Keep the new plants in pots (under cover in winter) for two years before planting out.

PRUNE Lemon verbena can grow leggy and lanky but responds well to a regular trim to keep it bushy in spring. Wait until new growth appears before cutting back all the previous year's growth to about 1½ in (4 cm). In summer, after the plant has flowered, trim off the flower heads down to the first or second set of leaves.

HARVEST

Lemon verbena leaves can be harvested between summer and late fall, right up until they begin to die back. In the first year after planting, only pick the occasional leaf. From the third year on, you can pick every other day if you wish.

USES

Lemon verbena is used to make a refreshing tea. It is often infused in oils and vinegars, and used in drinks and desserts including ice cream and rhubarb recipes. It also gives a fresh scent to a homemade glass cleaner made with vinegar, water, and a splash of dishwashing liquid.

Lemon verbena can lend its scent to homemade household cleaners.

Growing lemon verbena in a pot is a good way of displaying its handsome
architectural shape, as well as making it easy to move the plant to shelter in winter.

DILL *ANETHUM GRAVEOLENS*

PLANT TYPE Deciduous biennial or annual
HARDINESS Fully hardy
HEIGHT 20–40in (50cm–1m)
SPREAD 4–20in (10–50cm)
SOIL Any soil except clay
LIGHT ☼ ☼

Dill has finely divided, feathery foliage and tall, upright stems topped with sprays of small, yellowy acid-green flowers. The green leaves have a distinctive grassy scent and a refreshing taste with a hint of aniseed and citrus. The seeds have a stronger flavor and are also used in the kitchen.

Dill is happiest growing in well-drained soil kept evenly moist.

GROW AND MAINTAIN

Dill originally hails from southern Europe and western Asia. It is hardy and can withstand frost but hates a damp, cold situation and needs a sheltered position out of the wind; it prefers full sun but does not mind part shade. It grows best on slightly poor, well-drained soil, but will tolerate a range of conditions. Add sand to heavy soils before sowing or planting to improve the drainage.

Good cultivars to try for leaves include 'Domino', which reaches 24in (60cm) high, and 'Dukat', to 20in (50cm), a strong-growing type that is slower to bolt (run to flower) than others. 'Fernleaf' is a bushy variety, to around 18in (45cm), which is good for growing in containers, as is the dwarf type 'Bouquet', which reaches just 12in (30cm) and can be grown in small pots and even window boxes. It is also good for producing seeds, as is 'Mammoth', which grows to 3ft (90cm).

You can buy potted plants to grow on in the garden, or you can sow seed in two ways. The first option is to sow early under cover (or indoors on a windowsill) in late winter or early spring. Dill hates to have its roots disturbed, so grow in plug or cell trays or individual small modules, rather than in a seed tray where you would have to prick out seedlings later. When they are large enough to handle and all risk of frost has passed, harden seedlings off over a week, and then plant them out in the ground where they are to grow, spaced at least 8in (20cm) apart.

The second option is to sow seed directly in the garden in mid-spring, where the dill is to grow, in prepared soil in shallow drills. After about a

Dill flowers are decorative in the garden, and also produce strong-flavored seeds.

month, once the seedlings are large enough to handle, thin them out to around 6–8 in (15–20 cm) apart.

If sowing to grow in containers, use deep ones to give the roots space. Dill in pots may need staking, and won't last as long as ground-grown plants.

Repeat sow every 2 weeks throughout late spring and early summer to ensure a succession of plants to harvest throughout the growing season.

Keep soil moist, and water regularly in hot or dry periods to prevent the plants from bolting. This also helps stop bitterness from developing in the leaves of stressed plants. Keep the area around seedlings and plants free of weeds. Watch out for damage from slugs and aphids.

PROPAGATE If dill is allowed to flower, it will produce seed and self sow. Alternatively, you can collect the seed to sow yourself. However, you should be aware that the resulting seedlings of some cultivars may not "come true" and match the particular characteristics of the parent plant.

Raising seedlings in cells prevents root damage when planting out.

Clear away weeds from around the emerging dill seedlings.

PRUNE Dill will die back in autumn. If treating as an annual, you can discard the whole plant. If treating as a biennial, and growing on for a second year, cut back the stems and dead foliage.

HARVEST

Dill will produce leaves 6–10 weeks after sowing, for about eight weeks, and does best in late spring and early summer while the weather is still cool. However, if you sow successfully, cut back regularly, and keep well watered, you can enjoy dill right through to early fall. Snip or pick the leaves every few days once the plants have four or more leaves. Water well after harvesting. Remove developing flower stalks when you see them to prevent flowering and prolong leaf production.

If you want seeds, allow the plants to flower and seeds to ripen. Once ripe, cut the flower stalk and dry, head down, on newspaper or in a paper bag somewhere dry and warm for a week or two. Shake out the dried seed, and rub off any remaining husk, before storing in an airtight container.

To keep dill in leaf, remove whole stems as they begin to form flower heads.

Dill is added to the salt rub in curing salmon for gravlax.

USES

Dill is a culinary herb, with the leaves used most often for flavoring fish dishes. It is a favorite in northern European dishes like gravlax (salt-cured salmon) and potato salad, and also in the yogurt sauce that accompanies Greek dishes like souvlaki and kofta. Use fresh dill leaves raw, or chop up and freeze in a food storage bag for later use. The seeds are a key ingredient in curry powder and cucumber pickle recipes, and can be used to flavor bread.

CHERVIL *ANTHRISCUS CEREFOLIUM*

This hardy herb looks like a smaller version of cow parsley, its relative, and has pretty, bright green, ferny foliage and upright stems topped with clusters of tiny white flowers. The leaves taste like parsley with a mild licorice kick, and are a welcome fresh herb flavoring for winter dishes.

PLANT TYPE Deciduous biennial or annual
HARDINESS Fully hardy
HEIGHT Up to 24 in (60 cm)
SPREAD 12 in (30 cm)
SOIL Any light, well-drained soil
LIGHT ☼

GROW AND MAINTAIN

Anthriscus cerefolium is grown for its leaves, so although it is biennial, it's treated as annual—the leaves don't taste as good in its second year, when the plant puts its energy into flowering and setting seed.

With two or three sowings, chervil can be grown and harvested throughout the year, including during winter. Sow in early spring to get leaves in late spring and summer, and then sow in mid- and late summer for fall and winter harvests.

The plant likes cool conditions and will do best in light, moist but well-drained soil, preferably in part shade. Chervil will bolt during hot periods or in a position with too much sun, and this will affect vigor and flavor.

Chervil has a long, fragile taproot and hates disturbance. It does not respond well when transplanted,

Chervil leaves have a mild taste and are best used freshly picked.

If left unpicked, chervil will produce attractive, bright little flower heads.

so should be sown directly in the garden. Sow in spring once all risk of frost has passed, or at any time afterward until late summer. Sprinkle on top of moistened soil and firm in or cover lightly. When large enough to handle, thin seedlings out to 8 in (20 cm) apart. Alternatively, sow in containers, thinning out to one plant per pot.

Keep plants well watered. Remove developing flower stalks to encourage more leaf production. Lift and discard plants after four or more months of harvesting. Late-summer sowings will continue to produce leaves through winter if grown in a sheltered spot or protected with a cloche. Watch out for damage from aphids.

PROPAGATE Collect seed by letting the plant flower. Cut off the flower heads once they've turned brown, and dry them on newspaper or in a paper bag for a couple of weeks. Shake out or rub off the seeds, and either sow right

USES

Chervil works well with vegetable and egg dishes and salads, as well as with chicken and fish. It is one of the classic *fines herbes* and often part of a *bouquet garni* flavoring stews. Use raw, adding at the end of cooking.

Chervil is a perfect garnish for all kinds of omelet.

away or store them in a container or envelope somewhere dry and cool for up to a year. Chervil will also self-seed prolifically.

HARVEST

Leaves can be picked from 6–8 weeks after sowing, and will continue to be produced for up to five months. Harvest regularly for best results, cutting the leaves and using fresh, or freezing for later use.

LEAF CELERY

APIUM GRAVEOLENS SECALINUM GROUP

PLANT TYPE Deciduous biennial or annual
HARDINESS Fully hardy
HEIGHT 24 in (60 cm)
SPREAD 12 in (30 cm)
SOIL Fertile, sandy or loamy, well-drained
LIGHT ☼ ☼

Also known as cutting celery, par-cel, smallage, or Chinese celery, this herb looks like flat-leaf parsley with larger foliage. It is grown for its leaves and thin, hollow stalks, which taste and smell just like celery, and are an excellent substitute for that vegetable and much easier to grow.

GROW AND MAINTAIN

Several edible plants go under the species of *Apium graveolens*, including *A. graveolens* var. *dulce*, the vegetable stem celery; *A. graveolens* var. *rapaceum*, the root vegetable celeriac; and *A. graveolens* Secalinum Group, leaf celery. When sourcing seeds or plants, you may also find it labeled by one of its cultivar names such 'Par-cel' or 'Zwolsche Krul', or named as kintsai.

Leaf celery does not like conditions that are too hot or too cold. It is best grown in a sheltered position in full sun in spring and part shade in summer, in any light, well-drained soil. It is suitable for growing in containers.

Sow under cover in early spring and then transplant outside, or sow directly outdoors in mid to late spring, once all risk of frost has passed. Sprinkle seed on the surface of moistened seed starting mix or soil and gently press in. Seeds can take up to 3 weeks to germinate. Once large enough to handle, thin out seedlings to 8 in (20 cm) apart. Sow again in midsummer for continuous harvests through fall and winter. Keep well watered. Watch out for damage from rust.

PROPAGATE This biennial plant is usually grown as an annual herb, but if allowed to produce its small white flowers it will set seed. It will self-sow but you can also snip off flower heads (once they have turned brown), dry in a paper bag, and store for sowing the following year.

HARVEST

You can pick leaf celery beginning about a month after planting seedlings outdoors, or two months after direct sowing outside, and it will produce leaves for a few months. Harvest regularly to encourage the tastiest

Flower heads can be left to set seed, which is often used as a spicy flavoring.

young leaves and stalks, snipping stems off near the base. If the leaves have become old and tough, cut back the whole plant to about 6 in (15 cm) to encourage fresh growth.

USES

The leaves and stalks can be used in any recipes that call for parsley and celery. The stalks can be substituted for the celery in things like *mirepoix* or *soffritto* bases, soups, stocks, and sauces, and entire young sprigs are good chopped up for salads. Seeds can be used to make celery salt.

Leaf celery is tastiest when the leaves are young and picked regularly.

HORSERADISH *ARMORACIA RUSTICANA*

A tough, hardy, vigorous perennial, horseradish is very easy to grow. It has big, dock-like, green foliage and clusters of small, white summer flowers, but it is grown mostly for the large, white, fleshy roots. These taste hot and pungent and need to be handled with care to prevent eye irritation.

PLANT TYPE Deciduous perennial
HARDINESS Fully hardy
HEIGHT 30 in (75 cm)
SPREAD 18 in (45 cm)
SOIL Any fertile, well-drained soil
LIGHT ☼ ☀
WARNING! May cause eye irritation

Horseradish is very vigorous, so site carefully or plant in a pot to contain it.

The young leaves of horseradish can be used chopped in salads.

GROW AND MAINTAIN

You can grow horseradish from seed, but it is mostly available as pot-grown plants or pieces of root. It's not fussy about conditions but will grow best in deep, light, rich, moist but well-drained soil in full sun. It can become invasive so, in small gardens, grow in deep pots or raised beds to contain the spread.

Pot-grown plants are available all year but root pieces should be planted in early to mid-spring. Dig a hole about 4–6 in (10–12 cm) deep and wide, and sit the root in at a 45-degree angle. If roots or buds and shoots are visible at either end, place with roots at the bottom and shoots at the top. The top should sit about 1–2 in (3–5 cm) under the surface. Back-fill the planting hole with soil, and then water. Space plants or roots at least 12 in (30 cm) apart.

Keep plants moist and the soil around them clear of weeds while they establish. Apart from this, horseradish is fairly low-maintenance and not troubled by pests or diseases. Cut off leaves once they have died back in the fall. Fresh foliage will appear the following spring.

PROPAGATE Divide plants every two to three years in spring. Dig up a plant and cut the root into 6–8 in (15–20 cm) pieces. Replant immediately.

HARVEST

One-year-old roots are the best for eating, so dig up the whole plant carefully in its second fall, once the leaves have died back—usually after the first frosts—and separate the large main root from the smaller "thongs" or offshoot roots, which can be replanted. Wash the root and pat it dry. You can keep it fresh in a food storage bag in the fridge for a few months.

USES

Horseradish gives a kick to sauces, dips, and mayonnaise, and is often used in place of Japanese horseradish (a different species) to make wasabi. Fumes from the cut root can irritate the eye, so prepare in a well-ventilated space, and preferably peel or scrape pieces of root under water.

Cut off only as much root as you need and grate it to use fresh.

WORMWOOD *ARTEMISIA ABSINTHIUM*

Famous for its use in the alcoholic beverage absinthe, wormwood is an attractive ornamental garden plant as well as an herb. It creates a mound of deeply divided, gray-green to silver, aromatic leaves, and produces upright stems covered in small, round, yellow flowers in late summer.

PLANT TYPE Semi-evergreen subshrub
HARDINESS Fully hardy
HEIGHT 3 ft (1 m)
SPREAD 4 ft (1.2 m)
SOIL Any light, well-drained soil
LIGHT ☼
WARNING! Ingestion not advised

'Lambrook Silver' is a pretty and compact wormwood cultivar.

GROW AND MAINTAIN

Artemisia absinthium is a vigorous woody perennial, so choose the smaller, better-behaved cultivar 'Lambrook Silver' if growing as an ornamental feature. Wormwood should not be planted within 3 ft (1 m) of edible plants, as its roots secrete a chemical that inhibits their growth and affects the taste.

Wormwood prefers light, fertile, well-drained soil, and a position in full sun. 'Lambrook Silver' appreciates a sheltered spot. Wormwood is readily available as pot-grown plants but you can grow the species A. *absinthium* from seed. Sow indoors in spring on the surface of seed starting mix and barely cover. Use a rose attachment to water gently. Once seedlings emerge and have four or more leaves, prick out and pot on. Harden off seedlings and plant outside in their final position once all risk of frost has passed, spacing at least 24 in (60 cm) apart. Water plants as needed during the growing season.

PROPAGATE Divide established plants every three to four years in spring or fall. Take softwood cuttings in early summer.

Tiny yellow pompoms are borne on loose spikes in mid to late summer.

USES

The home gardener can use the dried leaves for potpourri and moth-repellent wardrobe sachets. Wormwood has a very bitter taste and contains strong chemical compounds, so it is not recommended for use in the kitchen, although it was traditionally used to flavor absinthe and other alcoholic drinks like vermouth. Planted in the garden, it will act as a barrier and help keep pests, from snails to deer, away from cherished plants.

PRUNE Wormwood can get leggy so, to encourage a good shape and fresh foliage, forgo the blooms and trim bushes back by up to half in summer. You can neaten up plants that have flowered by deadheading flower stems. To keep a plant within its allotted space, prune in early to mid-spring, removing dead or damaged stems and cutting back last year's growth to two leaves or buds from the old wood. Because wormwood can affect other plants, it's best not add prunings to the compost.

HARVEST

Harvest leaves any time from spring to early fall. Pick, dry in small bunches, and store in an airtight container. Wash hands after handling to remove the bitter taste it will leave on your fingers.

TARRAGON
ARTEMISIA DRACUNCULUS

This perennial herb is an upright, bushy plant, with slender stems lined with alternate, long, thin, pointed green leaves. It has a soft aroma and a distinct, strong anise flavor. It is used widely in French cooking and in herb mixes. Occasionally it may produce small, pendent, yellow flowers in summer.

PLANT TYPE Deciduous perennial
HARDINESS Half-hardy, fully hardy
HEIGHT Up to 36 in (90 cm)
SPREAD 18 in (45 cm)
SOIL Any light, well-drained soil
LIGHT ☼

Grow both in full sun in sandy or loamy, well-drained soil, as they hate to be wet, and prefer nutrient-poor, neutral soils to those that are heavy, rich, or acidic. They can also be planted in large containers, ideally with a growing mix of two parts sand to one part soil to ensure good drainage.

French tarragon seldom produces flowers or any viable seed. Suppliers may sometimes sell seed under the name of French tarragon, but these are probably Russian tarragon. The safest way to be sure of growing French tarragon is to buy young plants. Source them in spring, and plant out in a sheltered spot after all risk of frost. Place in the planting hole at the same depth that they were growing in the pots, level with the soil surface. Back-fill the planting hole and water in well. Space plants 18–24 in (45–60 cm) apart.

French tarragon leaves smell strongly when rubbed, unlike Russian tarragon.

Tarragon can be planted more closely in containers than in the ground.

GROW AND MAINTAIN

There are two types of tarragon available—French tarragon and Russian tarragon. They both go under the same botanical name, *Artemisia dracunculus*, and are too similar to tell apart by eye. French tarragon is considerably superior in taste, but is not fully hardy, while Russian tarragon is originally from Siberia and can cope with very cold, exposed situations, but it does not have much flavor.

Sow Russian tarragon seeds into pots or trays of seed starting mix in mid- to late spring, and place somewhere warm and sheltered. Prick out and pot on seedlings individually once they are large enough to handle, and plant out seedlings after hardening off, when all risk of frost has passed.

Water containers during the growing season, but plants in the ground should only need irrigation in very dry periods, as tarragon is quite drought-tolerant. Remove any flowers as they appear to encourage fresh leaf production.

Give French tarragon some extra protection in winter in cold or exposed gardens, with a deep, dry mulch around the base or by using a cloche.

Although perennial, these plants are only productive for up to four years, and should be replaced or divided to maintain flavor and vigor.

PROPAGATE Since French tarragon seldom produces seed, it is propagated by division or cuttings. Divide plants in spring, by lifting, splitting, and replanting the new sections immediately. Take softwood cuttings in summer. You can also dig up the underground runner roots in spring or fall, and pot them up individually to grow on somewhere frost-free over winter. These root cuttings are especially useful as a backup if you have plants in the ground that get hit hard by a bad winter.

PRUNE Trim all stems to near the base in late fall or early winter once foliage has died back. If not harvesting regularly, it may need to be cut back by up to half in summer to maintain a good shape and encourage fresh, tasty leaves.

HARVEST

Harvest leaves from late spring to early fall, cutting off stems with pruners or snips. The young leaves taste best. As well as using fresh, the leaves can also be dried or frozen.

Cutting tarragon regularly will ensure that the plant produces fresh leaves and doesn't become straggly.

USES

Tarragon is an essential ingredient in Bearnaise sauce, which is a classic accompaniment for steak, asparagus, and egg dishes. This herb is also the main flavoring in many creamy white wine sauces for fish, and in chicken tarragon, another classic French dish. It is used fresh in *fines herbes* and dried in *herbes de Provence* mixes. The fresh herb has the strongest anise flavor, while the dried is more subdued. Add to a bottle of vinegar to make tarragon vinegar for vibrant, quick salad dressings and vinaigrettes; the vinegar will also make a sweet-smelling homemade countertop cleaner or vegetable wash.

Tarragon vinegar is simply made by steeping a sprig in vinegar in a sterilized bottle or jar for a couple of weeks.

BORAGE *BORAGO*

Borage has large, rough, hairy, oval leaves, and fuzz-covered branching stems topped with clusters of small, star-shaped, brilliant blue blooms that taste like cucumber. The nectar-rich flowers are produced in abundance over a long period from summer into fall, and are very attractive to pollinators.

PLANT TYPE Annual, deciduous perennial
HARDINESS Fully hardy
HEIGHT 24 in (60 cm)
SPREAD 12 in (30 cm)
SOIL Any well-drained soil
LIGHT ☼ ☀
WARNING! May cause skin irritation

Borage's delicate blue flowers make it an ornamental as well as useful plant.

GROW AND MAINTAIN

Also known as starflower, the most widely available borage is the species *Borago officinalis*, an annual that grows up to 24 in (60 cm) high, and has mostly blue but occasionally pink starry flowers. There is also a white-flowered

Young borage leaves can be used fresh in salads.

cultivar called 'Alba', and a rare variety with two-tone foliage called 'Variegata'. *B. officinalis* is very easy to grow and is not fussy about conditions, tolerating any well-drained soil in full sun or partial shade. Ideally it grows best in poor, light soil in full sun.

Sow seed outdoors in spring, after all risk of frost has passed, directly where you want borage to grow, as it doesn't like being transplanted. Make a shallow hole or drill to around 2 in (5 cm) deep, sprinkle seed thinly, and cover with soil before watering. Once seedlings are large enough to handle, thin out to 12–18 in (30–45 cm) apart.

'Alba' is a borage cultivar with pretty, white, starry blooms.

Borage is quite drought-tolerant, so although young plants should be kept moist while establishing, you can then let the soil dry out between waterings. It does not need extra feeding. Watch out for powdery mildew—lift and destroy any affected plants.

Deadhead spent flowers to encourage more to form throughout the season. Borage self-sows prolifically, so removing spent flowers also has the advantage of stopping the plant from spreading itself too extensively. When the foliage starts to die back in late fall or early winter, lift plants and discard on the compost heap. You may wish to cut

Borage is one of the most pollinator-friendly plants you can grow; bees in particular love its nectar-rich flowers.

Borage flowers and leaves are often used in salads and cold summer dishes to add a subtle but refreshing cucumber note. The flowers are a common flavoring for drinks including Pimm's cups and gin cocktails, either as a garnish or frozen into ice cubes. They can also be crystallized or candied for use in cakes and confectionery.

The leaves can be used as you would spinach: raw when young and, as the older leaves get tougher and less palatable, cooked in soups and other hot dishes.

In the garden, borage makes a lovely ornamental flower and a great companion plant for fruit and vegetables, helping to draw in pollinators, especially bees.

Freeze borage flowers in ice trays to make decorative ice cubes.

off and throw away the seed heads separately as this will also prevent borage from spreading through self-sowing when the compost is used.

As well as annual borage, there is also a lesser-known, low-growing perennial variety called *B. pygmaea*, known as prostrate or Corsican borage. This grows to around 18 in (45 cm) and has delicate, bell-shaped, light blue flowers in summer. It is available as potted plants, is hardy, and will come back every year. It prefers moist but well-drained soil in full sun or partial shade. Prostrate borage makes a wonderful ground cover.

PROPAGATE Allow borage plants to flower, set seed, and self-sow before cutting down, or collect the seed in paper bags once the flower head has turned brown. Store seed somewhere cool and dry, and sow directly the following spring.

HARVEST

Borage will produce leaves and flowers to harvest 8–10 weeks after sowing, and if regularly picked or deadheaded will continue right up until late fall. Pick flowers to use fresh, to freeze, or to dry, just after they have opened.

Harvest young leaves anytime, pinching them off at the base, and use fresh. It is best to wear gloves if handling older, bristly leaves and stems as the prickles can irritate the skin.

POT MARIGOLD

CALENDULA OFFICINALIS

Pot marigolds have softly fuzzy, fragrant leaves and pretty, daisylike blooms with edible petals. The flowers come in vibrant shades of orange, as well as yellow, cream, and occasionally pink, and brighten up the garden over a long period from early summer, sometimes until the frosts.

PLANT TYPE Annual
HARDINESS Fully hardy
HEIGHT 12–24 in (30–60 cm)
SPREAD Up to 24 in (60 cm)
SOIL Any light well-drained soil
LIGHT ☼ ☼

Colorful blooms are produced throughout summer and fall.

Pot marigolds are helpful companion plants when grown with other crops.

GROW AND MAINTAIN

Calendula officinalis is an easy, quick-growing annual herb with prolific orange flowers. The most popular cultivar is 'Indian Prince', which reaches 24 in (60 cm) and has deeper orange blooms with darker reverses. 'Neon' is larger and a darker, red-orange; and Fiesta Gitana Group has double flowers in yellow and orange. 'Snow Princess' is an unusual type, growing to just 12 in (30 cm) with pale-yellow to cream blooms.

Pot marigolds will grow in any well-drained soil in full sun or partial shade, but hate heavy, wet conditions and prefer poor, light soil in a sunny spot. Sow seed either in fall under cover, or direct in spring once the risk of frost has passed.

Sprinkle the seeds on the surface, cover with ½ in (1 cm) of soil, and water well. Thin out seedlings, once they appear, to one per pot or spaced out to 12 in (30 cm) apart in the ground. Those that were started off under cover can be hardened off once the risk of frost has passed in spring and transplanted into their final position.

Keep plants well watered while they establish, and then reduce to occasional watering when necessary. On young plants, watch out for damage from slugs. Pinch out the growing tips to encourage the plants to grow more bushy and compact: using pruners or your fingers, take stems back to the next set of leaves. Deadhead spent flowers to keep the plants producing blooms all season.

PROPAGATE If you allow the flowers to die back and set seed, pot marigolds will self-sow quite extensively, or you can collect the seed. Seed from named cultivars of *Calendula officinalis* probably will not "come true" and so may not match the parent plant in particular characteristics.

HARVEST

Pot marigolds will produce flowers from within two months of a spring sowing, and can be harvested continuously until fall. Pick the blooms in the late morning. You can use the petals fresh immediately, or dry them and store in an airtight container.

USES

Pot marigold petals have a slightly peppery taste. They are used fresh and dried, raw and cooked, as a flavoring and a garnish for salads and soups, infused into oil, or made into tea. Fold them into the mix for cookies or sweet buns, or use as a saffron substitute to color rice dishes. They make a yellow dye, and are also often utilized in soothing skin balms. In the garden, they will lure aphids away from other plants and attract beneficial ladybugs and hoverflies.

CARAWAY *CARUM CARVI*

Caraway is an upright plant with finely divided, fragrant green leaves, and tall stems topped with flat clusters of tiny white flowers in summer. These blooms are followed by pungent, aromatic fruits, referred to as seeds, that have a licorice-like flavor.

PLANT TYPE Deciduous biennial
HARDINESS Fully hardy
HEIGHT Up to 24 in (60 cm)
SPREAD 12 in (30 cm)
SOIL Any well-drained soil
LIGHT ☼ ☼

GROW AND MAINTAIN

Caraway is a biennial plant that produces feathery leaves in its first season, reaching a height of around 8–12 in (20–30 cm), and in its second season also sends up flower stalks to 24 in (60 cm). It blooms with many small white or pinkish florets, which die back and set lots of hard brown fruits—usually called seeds—which are the main reason caraway is grown.

It will grow in any fertile, well-drained soil in sun or part shade, and will tolerate heavier soils, but prefers a humus-rich, sandy loam in full sun. You may need to add organic matter to improve the soil where you want the caraway to grow.

Caraway develops a long, fragile taproot and hence does not respond well to transplanting. This means it is best to sow directly outdoors where you want it to grow, in fall or in spring after all risk of frost has passed. Sprinkle seed into shallow drills, cover thinly and water. It can take a few weeks to sprout. Once they are large enough to handle, thin seedlings out to 8–12 in (20–30 cm) apart.

Keep the soil around young plants moist and clear of weeds, watering regularly at the base of the plant, being careful not to splash the leaves or stems. Once established, reduce the watering to only when the soil looks too dry. At the end of the first growing season, cut back the foliage to near the base. Mulch around the plants to offer extra protection for winter. Once the plant has set seed, you can lift and discard on the compost heap if you wish.

PROPAGATE Caraway will self-sow if allowed, and you can also collect the seed to sow (see Harvest, right). To maintain a continual harvest every season, sow more seed every year.

Caraway produces flowers only in its second year.

USES

Caraway seeds are used to flavor bread, especially rye, as well as cheeses, cabbage dishes, and Indian cuisine. They can be chewed raw to aid digestion. Add leaves to salads raw or cook with them as you would parsley. The root can be prepared and eaten as you would a parsnip or other root vegetable.

Caraway seeds have a distinctive, sharp aniseed flavor.

HARVEST

Pick the leaves sparingly any time during the growing season. Harvest seeds when flowers have died back and gone brown. Chop off the flower head and place in a paper bag for several days. Shake to knock the seed off into the bag. Pick out the seeds from the chaff and use, store, or sow. The root can be harvested once the plant has set seed.

CORNFLOWER *CENTAUREA CYANUS*

Also known as bachelors' buttons and blue bottle, this herb is grown for its pretty, thistlelike blooms, which have edible petals in blue, and sometimes in pastel shades of white, pink, and purple, too. Easy to grow and low-maintenance, it will thrive in almost any sunny situation.

PLANT TYPE Annual
HARDINESS Fully hardy
HEIGHT Up to 30 in (75 cm)
SPREAD Up to 8 in (20 cm)
SOIL Any well-drained soil
LIGHT ☼

GROW AND MAINTAIN

Centaurea cyanus produces an abundance of blue flowers from early or midsummer right through into early fall. It is often available in mixed seed packs with different colors together, such as the Polka Dot Series, but individual cultivars worth seeking out include the double 'Blue Boy', and 'Red Boy', which has blooms of deepest pink. There is also a variety sold as 'White' or 'White Ball' that opens pure white before developing a pale pink center. 'Black Ball' is an extraordinary variety with double flowers in rich dark purple to maroon.

Annual cornflowers are not fussy and will grow in any well-drained soil, even tolerating heavy clay and poor or chalky ground. However, they do need a position in full sun. They are hardy

Cornflowers will tolerate all kinds of tough growing situations.

'Blue Boy' is a popular tall-growing cornflower cultivar.

annuals and will grow easily from seed sown in early spring or in fall. Scatter seed onto prepared soil where you want plants to grow, or sow in drills ½ in (1 cm) deep and cover lightly before watering. Thin out seedlings to at least 8 in (20 cm) apart once they are large enough to handle. You can also grow cornflowers easily in containers.

Keep plants moist to prolong flowering throughout the season, and deadhead regularly to encourage more blooms to form. Tall plants may need staking. At the end of the season, lift and discard plants as they fade.

PROPAGATE Cornflowers will self-sow prolifically, so allow them to set seed or collect the seed to store and sow the following season.

HARVEST

Sow in spring for flowers in around 10 weeks, from midsummer, or in the fall for blooms early the next summer. Pick the flowers as they open and use fresh, or tie into small bunches and dry.

Bees and other pollinators are particularly attracted to cornflowers.

USES

Cornflower petals have a mild, spicy-sweet, clove-like flavor and are used fresh as a colorful garnish for salads, fruity desserts, cakes, and cocktails. They are used dry as a tea, in potpourri, and as an eco-friendly confetti for celebrations. In the garden they are popular in colorful wildflower-meadow-style plantings of annuals, and as cut flowers, and make excellent pollinator plants to attract bees, butterflies, and hoverflies to fruit and vegetable plants.

Many cornflower seed mixes produce flowers in a variety of complementary pastel shades.

CHAMOMILE *CHAMAEMELUM NOBILE*

Chamomile is a low-growing, mat-forming, hardy evergreen perennial herb, with feathery, fernlike green leaves that release a delicious, strong fragrance of fresh apples when crushed or brushed past. It is also grown for its small, daisy-like flowers, which appear over a long period through summer.

PLANT TYPE Evergreen perennial
HARDINESS Fully hardy
HEIGHT Up to 12 in (30 cm)
SPREAD 18 in (45 cm)
SOIL Any well-drained soil
LIGHT ☼ ☼

Chamomile flowers, like the foliage, have a sweet, floral taste and fragrance like that of crisp apples.

GROW AND MAINTAIN

Chamaemelum nobile, known as Roman chamomile, is a creeping plant which grows to around 10 in (25 cm), with finely divided, sweetly scented foliage and white flowers with yellow centers. The cultivar 'Flore Pleno' is a double-flowered form with pretty pompom blooms in creamy white. It is more compact, growing to 4–6 in (10–15 cm). 'Treneague', known as lawn chamomile, is a nonflowering form that reaches just 2¼ in (6 cm), and is an excellent ground cover and the best choice for chamomile lawns and seats (see p.24).

'Flore Pleno' is a compact, spreading cultivar that makes pretty ground cover.

Make a chamomile lawn by planting the mat-forming cultivar 'Treneague'.

There are two other plants often called chamomile—dyer's chamomile, *Anthemis tinctoria*, and German chamomile, *Matricaria recutita*. Both are taller-growing than Roman chamomile, and not used in the same way.

Roman chamomile will grow in any well-drained soil in full sun or part shade, but does not like wet or heavy conditions and prefers a sunny, sheltered spot. It can be grown from seed. In spring, sow seed onto the surface of pots of seed starting mix and firm in gently. If sowing in early spring you may need to use a heated propagator to get seeds to germinate. When large enough to handle, thin seedlings or prick out into individual pots to grow on. After all risk of frost has passed, harden off and transplant out to their final positions. Alternatively, in late spring, sow direct where they are to grow, scattering the seed onto prepared soil and watering in.

Named cultivars such as 'Flore Pleno' and 'Treneague' cannot be grown from seed, and are usually sourced as plugs or plants. Plant out in spring, placing the plants so the surface of the soil is the

Lawn chamomile clumps are easy to divide by hand for propagation.

same level as they were growing in the pot. Space 8–12 in (20–30 cm) apart, or closer for a chamomile lawn or seat, to 4–6 in (10–15 cm) apart. Water in well.

Keep the area around the plants clear of weeds while they establish, and keep plants watered during dry periods.

Harvest flowers regularly or deadhead spent blooms to encourage more to form. Feed established plants with a general liquid fertilizer from spring to fall.

PRUNE Chamomile should be trimmed regularly to keep a compact form and prevent plants getting leggy. After flowering types have bloomed, cut them back hard to around 2 in (5 cm).

PROPAGATE Roman chamomile will set seed if flowers are allowed to fade on the plant. This can be collected and stored to sow the following spring. Named cultivars can be propagated through division in the fall or spring. Simply dig up a clump and pull apart into smaller sections, which can then be planted further apart, or used to fill gaps. It is a good idea to divide these plants every three years to promote healthy growth and control their spread. You can also take cuttings from established plants in spring or fall.

Pick chamomile flower heads as soon as they open for best flavor.

HARVEST

Flowers can be harvested throughout the summer. Pick off the flower heads once they are open. Use fresh or lay them to dry on a rack or wire tray somewhere dry and warm indoors for several days. Store in an airtight container out of direct light.

Chamomile tea can be made with fresh or dried flowers.

USES

Chamomile flowers are used to make a calming tea, often with lemon and honey. Make leaves and flowers into a soothing, scented herb pillow, or dry to add to potpourri. In the garden, use to make an aromatic lawn or seat.

CHICORY *CICHORIUM INTYBUS*

Chicory has toothed or divided leaves and wiry, branching stems lined with starry flowers, which are usually clear sky-blue in color, but sometimes pink or white; they last only one day but are produced over a long period. Chicory is grown for its thick, fleshy taproot and bitter-tasting leaves.

PLANT TYPE Deciduous perennial
HARDINESS Fully hardy
HEIGHT 3–4 ft (1–1.2 m)
SPREAD 12 in (30 cm)
SOIL Any well-drained soil
LIGHT ☼

Chicory is sometimes grown for its numerous decorative flowers.

Sugarloaf chicory is grown for its lettuce-like leaves.

GROW AND MAINTAIN

Common chicory, *Cichorium intybus*, comes in two different types. Root chicory, *C. intybus* var. *sativum*, is grown for its large root; the cultivar 'Magdeburg' is particularly noted for good root size and quality. Other varieties of *C. intybus* are grown for their leaves, including radicchio and sugarloaf chicory, and for "chicons," forced or blanched leaves treated as a vegetable, such as witloof chicory.

Chicory is easy to grow—it is often found naturalized on roadside verges and in hedgerows—and will grow in any fertile, well-drained soil in full sun.

However, for best results, it prefers a light soil that is neutral to alkaline, and does not like clay or acidic soil.

Sow seed under cover in late summer or fall, planting out seedlings the following spring after all risk of frost, or directly sow where they are to grow in spring. Ensure the soil is kept evenly moist to encourage germination. Seedlings should emerge within a few weeks. Plant or thin seedlings out to 12 in (30 cm) apart.

PROPAGATE Allow plants to flower and set seed. Collect seed and sow fresh, or store it somewhere dry and sow direct the following spring.

HARVEST

Chicory leaves can be harvested once the plant grows to more than 12 in (30 cm) high. Pick leaves young, before flowering, to eat fresh. Roots will be ready for harvesting in late summer, after flowering. It is best to harvest one-season roots as they will become woody in their second season. Dig deep around the plant to lift out the whole large root without breaking it.

USES

Chicory root is used to make a nutty-flavored hot drink, used for centuries as a substitute for coffee. Clean the fresh roots, slice them, dry, roast, and then grind them up and add to hot water. They can also be used to flavor beer. Young roots can be lifted and eaten like parsnips. The leaves can be eaten raw in salads, or cooked to reduce the bitter flavor.

Cut chicory root into small, evenly-sized pieces before roasting.

THAI LIME *CITRUS HYSTRIX*

Also known as makrut lime, this tropical herb is a dwarf citrus tree grown for its aromatic, dark green, glossy leaves, which are two-part or double in form and shaped like an hourglass. They also have thorny stems and fragrant white or pink flowers followed by knobbly-skinned green fruit.

PLANT TYPE Evergreen shrub
HARDINESS Tender
HEIGHT Up to 5 ft (1.5 m) when grown indoors in a pot
SPREAD Up to 28 in (70 cm) when grown indoors in a pot
SOIL Loam-based, well-drained soil
LIGHT ☼

Both leaves and flowers, produced all year, are strongly perfumed.

GROW AND MAINTAIN

Thai lime is not hardy and needs protection from frost, so should be grown under cover somewhere light, such as a greenhouse or conservatory, or as a houseplant on a bright windowsill for most of the year. Pots can be placed out in the garden in a sunny spot in summer and brought back inside before the first frosts in fall.

Plants are available as small bushes, usually in 1- or 2-liter pots. Pot on into a larger display container that has excellent drainage, or—if your preferred decorative pot does not have a hole at the bottom—into a larger plastic pot, which can be easily popped in and out of the bigger display container in order to water, feed, and care for the plant.

Ensure good drainage by adding a layer of pebbles to the base of the container before potting on. Ready-made citrus potting mixes are a great option for beginners; alternatively, use a commercial potting mix, adding some sterilized topsoil and perlite.

Give plants plenty of light and a steady, cool temperature of around 60–64°F (16–18°C), in a sheltered draft-free area away from direct heat sources such as vents. Keep moist but not wet, allowing the top of the soil to dry out between waterings, especially in winter. If your home is dry, mist the leaves with water every week. Feed monthly with citrus plant food from spring to fall. Repot every couple of years in spring.

PROPAGATE Pot-grown Thai lime is best propagated via semi-hardwood cuttings in late summer.

PRUNE On larger shrubs, remove any dead, damaged, diseased, or crossing and rubbing branches in winter or early spring, when you can also trim back your plant all over if you wish to keep a more compact form. Watch out for the sharp thorns while handling the stems.

HARVEST

Pick a few leaves regularly to encourage constant growth. They can be used fresh, or dried or frozen for future use. Store fresh leaves in a jar for up to one week, or in a food storage bag in the

USES

Thai lime leaves give a unique, bright, citrus kick to southeast Asian cuisine including curries, soups, rice dishes, spice paste, and stir-fries. Leaves are either added whole and removed before serving, or shredded up or crushed, to release the aromatic oils, and left in. Pull or cut out the rib of the leaf before using. The fruit is sometimes also used for its juice or zest.

Leaves can be left whole or shredded very finely for flavoring.

fridge or freezer for up to a year. Leaves can be dried by hanging upside down in a warm, dry, shaded place. Store in an airtight jar for up to two years. Fruit is occasionally produced throughout the year, and begins to yellow when ripe.

CORIANDER *CORIANDRUM SATIVUM*

Coriander is grown for its highly aromatic, divided leaves, which are pungent and tartly refreshing in flavor, and its seeds. All parts of the plant are edible, including the clusters of white or pale pink flowers; the seeds that follow have a spicy flavor with a citrus hint.

PLANT TYPE Deciduous annual
HARDINESS Tender
HEIGHT Up to 27 in (70 cm)
SPREAD Up to 12 in (30 cm)
SOIL Any light, well-drained soil
LIGHT ☼ ☼

GROW AND MAINTAIN

Coriander leaves—also known as cilantro—are scallop-shaped at the base when young, becoming feathery higher up the stem and as they grow. The species *Coriandrum sativum*, which reaches about 20 in (50 cm), is good for leaf production, but the widely available cultivars 'Leisure' and 'Calypso' are more vigorous, with lots of leaves, and are slower to bolt. Unusual varieties include 'Lemon', which has leaves with a citrusy flavor and fragrance; and 'Confetti', which has very finely divided, ferny leaves. 'Morocco' has pale pink flowers and grows slightly taller, to around 27 in (70 cm), and is the best option to grow for seeds.

You can grow coriander indoors in a pot on a windowsill, but it will not be at its best in this situation. It prefers to grow outdoors, somewhere not too warm, in late spring and through summer. It will bolt very quickly in direct, hot sun, so choose a situation where your plants will receive bright morning sun but shade in the afternoon. Coriander needs light, very well-drained, preferably sandy soil. If growing in containers, use potting mix for citrus with added perlite or sand to improve drainage.

You can start seeds off under cover in early spring in small pots, and plant seedlings outside once all risk of frost

Coriander 'Leisure' is a strong-growing, bushy cultivar that can be relied on for prolific leaf production.

In hot, sunny conditions, coriander quickly bolts (runs to flower and seed).

Sow coriander seed directly in drills in the ground for best results.

Coriander needs watering regularly to keep it moist but not too wet.

USES

Coriander leaves and seeds are used widely in many cuisines, especially in Indian, Thai, Middle Eastern, and Mexican dishes, such as curries, dips, salsas, salads, and soups. Leaves are used fresh, either raw for cold dishes or added at the very end of cooking, just before serving. The leaf stalks hold tons of flavor and can be added before or during cooking. Dried seeds can be used whole or ground.

Coriander leaf is best added just after cooking for maximum flavor.

has passed. However, since coriander develops a large root, it does not always transplant well and may react by bolting quickly after being moved. The best method is to sow direct in spring where plants are to grow in the garden, once all risk of frost has passed. Create a shallow drill and water the soil before sowing the seed thinly and covering over lightly. Keep the soil moist and shoots should appear in 7–10 days. Once they are large enough to handle, thin seedlings out to around 6 in (15 cm) apart. Coriander bolts easily, and once a plant has begun flowering, the leaves will not be as palatable to eat. For a continual supply of more tasty, fresh leaves, sow in succession every fortnight to a month.

Coriander hates damp and humid conditions, but will also bolt if it is allowed to dry out, so try to keep the soil just moist but not wet. Feed with general liquid fertilizer every few weeks. To have really bushy plants, pinch out the tips often, or simply harvest regularly.

Once plants have flowered, either use them for seed or dig them up and discard on the compost heap.

PROPAGATE Collect seed when ripe after flowering, dry, and store to sow the following spring.

HARVEST

Leaves can be harvested from around midsummer, once plants have reached over 4 in (10 cm) tall. Picking constantly encourages the plant to produce more leaves. Put bunches of cut leaves with stalks in a glass of cold water—as you would a bunch of flowers—to keep fresh in the fridge for up to 2 weeks. Alternatively, wash and dry completely, and wrap in paper towel or a clean cotton cloth, before placing in an airtight storage box or food storage bag. Leaves and stalks can also be chopped up or blended and frozen in olive oil in ice cube trays.

To harvest seeds, allow the plants to flower and seeds to form. Once they begin to turn brown, cover the flower heads with a paper bag to contain the seeds, tie the bag at the base, cut the stems, and hang upside down somewhere warm and dry for 1–2 weeks. Shake out the seeds and store in an airtight container.

Cut coriander stems often to promote the growth of new leaves.

LEMONGRASS *CYMBOPOGON CITRATUS*

This tropical herb is a grassy plant cultivated for its cane-like stems, which swell toward the bottom. The core of this leaf base has a strong citrus aroma and a lemony flavor. It is a vigorous, clump-forming perennial with arching blue-green leaves and occasionally sprays of pinky-green flowers.

PLANT TYPE Evergreen or semi-evergreen perennial
HARDINESS Tender
HEIGHT Up to 3 ft (1 m) in a pot
SPREAD Up to 20 in (50 cm) in a pot
SOIL Loam-based, well-drained soil
LIGHT ☼

Lemongrass is tender and so best planted in pots under cover or indoors.

GROW AND MAINTAIN

Lemongrass comes from southern Asia, and is not suitable for growing outside in the ground all year round in cool temperate climates. It is best raised in containers under cover or indoors as a houseplant by a bright window. It can be placed outside in a sunny, sheltered spot in summer.

Cymbopogon citratus, West Indian lemongrass, is the most common variety grown for culinary use. It likes enriched, well-drained potting mix in full light, and to be hot and humid in summer but warm and dry in winter.

You can buy plants, or grow your own from seed. In spring, sow thinly on the surface of moist seed starting mix in pots and firm in gently. Place in a heated propagator until they germinate, usually within three weeks, then thin out to one per pot and put somewhere light and warm. Keep soil moist, placing the pot in a saucer to irrigate from below.

Repot seedlings into larger containers when roots appear at the bottom of the pot; when this happens again, plant in their final display pot, which should be at least 12 in (30 cm) wide and high. Keep the soil moist, and mist the leaves. Feed regularly in spring and summer.

In winter, water the pot occasionally. Lemongrass is evergreen but can go dormant, with foliage turning brown. Cut off dead leaves in spring, and refresh the top layer of soil in the pot.

PROPAGATE Fresh shoots sold for cooking can root successfully (see p.37). You can also take cuttings from a mature plant. Once it becomes too large for its container, divide in spring.

PRUNE In the fall, trim back leafy top growth on indoor-grown container plants to about 4 in (10 cm) above where the stems swell.

HARVEST

Seed-sown plants will be ready in about 3–4 months. Use stalks that are at least ½ in (1 cm) in diameter at the base, cutting beneath the white swollen section. Use fresh, or wrap in plastic wrap and refrigerate for 2–3 weeks. You can also freeze stalks for up to six months or dry them and store in an airtight container for up to a year.

USES

Lemongrass leaves can be used to make tea, but it is the stalk that is mostly used, fresh, to flavor southeast Asian cuisine including Thai, Vietnamese, and Cambodian dishes such as curries, salads, and soups. The inside of the stalk is soft and tasty, but the rest is very fibrous, so stems are typically bruised or crushed with the side of a knife, used whole in the dish, and then removed after cooking. Alternatively, stalks can be peeled and then sliced up.

Stems of lemongrass are used fresh for their fragrant citrus flavor.

ARUGULA *DIPLOTAXIS* AND *ERUCA*

Also known as rocket, these herbs are grown for their arrow-shaped, green leaves, which have a distinct peppery zing that gets hotter with age. Both arugula species are fast-growing, low-maintenance, and versatile plants that also produce four-petaled white or yellow flowers.

PLANT TYPE Deciduous perennial, annual
HARDINESS Half-hardy
HEIGHT Up to 12 in (60 cm)
SPREAD 8 in (20 cm)
SOIL Any well-drained soil
LIGHT ☼ ☼

Arugula flowers can be picked and used as a decorative and spicy garnish

GROW AND MAINTAIN

There are two main types of arugula, garden arugula and wild arugula, though there is often confusion over their naming and identification at point of sale. *Eruca vesicaria* subsp. *sativa*, also known as garden, salad, or herb arugula, is an annual with larger, more rounded leaves and a mildly nutty, peppery flavor. *Diplotaxis tenuifolia* is usually sold as wild arugula; this plant is also often found under the name of *Rucola selvatica*. It is a perennial with stronger-tasting, narrower, serrated leaves. It will tolerate some sun in summer, but both types, if grown in full sun, do best in the cooler temperatures of spring and fall. They will bolt quickly in the heat in summer, when they should be grown in part shade. The leaves become hotter and more bitter after bolting and as they mature.

Arugula can be grown from seed, or bought as plugs or small plants and then planted out in any well-drained soil in spring, once all risk of frost has passed. Sow seeds thinly, direct where they are to grow, in shallow holes or drills and cover lightly. Once they are large enough to handle, thin out seedlings to around 6–8 in (15–20 cm) apart. Sow more seed every 3–4 weeks to create a continual harvest.

Keep plants well watered. There is no need to feed any variety of arugula. Discard annual plants on the compost heap at the end of the growing season. Protect perennial plants over winter with horticultural fleece or a cloche, or you can treat them as annuals or biennials and sow fresh plants every year or two.

PROPAGATE Both types of arugula are best propagated through seed and will self-sow readily.

USES

Arugula leaves add a spicy kick to salads, including mesclun, and are used as a peppery garnish on pizza and tarts. They make a fine pesto sauce. They can also be added to cooked dishes such as pasta, quiche, and risotto, or used to make arugula soup. Flowers and seeds are also edible but the seeds are very hot.

Fresh arugula with Parmesan is a classic salad combination.

HARVEST

Plants can be ready to harvest within 6–8 weeks of sowing. Cut or pick off the outer leaves regularly to prevent flowering and ensure a steady supply of fresh growth.

FENNEL *FOENICULUM VULGARE*

Fennel has tall, branching stems with clouds of aromatic, ferny, green or purple-brown foliage, and flat-topped clusters of small yellow flowers, followed by long, thin, green to brown seeds. Both the leaves and seeds smell and taste of aniseed. Fennel blooms are very attractive to pollinators.

PLANT TYPE Deciduous perennial
HARDINESS Fully hardy
HEIGHT Up to 6 ft (1.8 m)
SPREAD Up to 20 in (50 cm)
SOIL Any well-drained soil
LIGHT ☼ ☼

Fennel produces a mass of attractive feathery foliage with a strong aniseed flavor and scent.

The handsome foliage of bronze fennel makes it a popular ornamental.

GROW AND MAINTAIN

The herb fennel, *Foeniculum vulgare*, is not to be confused with its relative Florence fennel, *F. vulgare* var. *azoricum*, which is grown as an annual for its bulblike stems that are harvested as a vegetable. *F. vulgare*, common fennel, does not develop bulbs. It is an upright, short-lived perennial, with feathery foliage. The cultivar 'Purpureum', known as bronze fennel and also sold as 'Bronze' or 'Rubrum', has purple-bronze foliage. It is just as tasty as the green type, but is so attractive it is often used as an ornamental garden

Snip off spent flower heads if you don't want fennel to self sow.

plant as well as an herb. Other bronze-leaved varieties to seek out include 'Giant Bronze' and 'Smoky'.

Fennel likes a sheltered, sunny situation, and will grow in any well-drained soil, but will be lush and happy in fertile, moist but well-drained conditions. You can sow seeds in early spring under cover in modules or small pots of seed starting mix, and transplant seedlings to their final growing position once all risk of frost has passed. However, fennel develops large roots and tends not to like to be disturbed, so the ideal method is to sow direct where it is to grow in mid to late spring. You can also sow seed later, in summer.

Beneficial insects, such as hoverflies, love fennel flower heads.

Fennel makes a profusion of seeds if allowed to flower.

Water regularly while young, but be careful not to waterlog plants; they can be quite drought-tolerant once they are established. Fennel is generally a low-maintenance, easy-care plant that does not require much attention, but watch out for damage to young plants from snails, slugs, and aphids.

It self-sows freely and can become invasive, so if you are growing it for leaves, snip off the flower heads to stop it from seeding around. Try not to grow green and bronze types together or near similar plants like dill, as cross-pollination can adversely affect the flavor of the resulting seed and the color and flavor of the foliage of next year's new plants.

In fall or winter, remove dead foliage and cut stems down to the base. Fresh growth will appear in spring.

PROPAGATE Collect ripe seed after flowering and sow immediately or store until spring.

HARVEST

Pick leaves continuously from early summer through to early fall. They will stay fresh in the fridge in a food storage bag for a couple of days, or you can freeze chopped leaves in ice cubes for several months.

USES

Fennel leaves are often used for fish dishes and sauces as well as dips and curries. The seeds can be used to flavor bread, ice cream, and chutneys, and are an important ingredient in spice mixes, including Chinese five spice and garam masala. Both leaves and seeds are used to infuse oils and vinegars.

Dry-roasting releases the aromatic oils in fennel seeds.

Seeds can be dried for culinary use. After flowering, cut off the seed heads and place in a paper bag. Hang upside down to dry for a couple of weeks somewhere warm and dry. Store seeds in an airtight container for up to a year.

Fennel attracts a host of wildlife, including swallowtail butterfly caterpillars.

SWEET WOODRUFF

GALIUM ODORATUM

This perennial herb is a vigorous, mat-forming woodlander that likes shady, moist places. It produces upright stems circled with collars of whorled green leaves, which have a fresh, sweet fragrance, topped with clusters of star-shaped, white blooms in late spring and early summer.

PLANT TYPE Deciduous perennial
HARDINESS Fully hardy
HEIGHT Up to 12 in (30 cm)
SPREAD 12 in (30 cm) or more
SOIL Any well-drained soil
LIGHT ☼ ☼

The starry flowers of sweet woodruff make a most attractive ground cover.

GROW AND MAINTAIN

Also known as sweet-scented bedstraw and kiss me quick, *Galium odoratum* is an aromatic plant often used as a ground cover, particularly under trees. It needs space to grow and spreads easily, so is more suitable for naturalizing in woodland schemes or given some room in a shady area to block out weeds rather than placed in borders or containers.

Sweet woodruff is not fussy, and will tolerate a broad range of conditions, growing in light or heavy and acid or alkaline soils. However, it will not do well in full sun, and ideally prefers a rich, loamy, moist but well-drained soil.

Buy plants or start from seed, direct sowing where it is to grow in early spring. Scatter seeds over the prepared area and cover lightly with sifted soil. Water in well.

Sweet woodruff is a very easy plant with little maintenance required, but can become invasive so do not feed or water unless necessary. It can become dormant in very hot, dry conditions, but will revive when watered. The top growth will die back in fall and can then be removed.

PROPAGATE Sweet woodruff spreads quickly by its roots, and through self-sowing. Divide mature plants in the fall or spring. Simply dig up a clump, making sure there are roots attached, and transplant half of it to a different area.

PRUNE If you have a large swathe away from tree roots that you would like to control, it can be cut back occasionally with a lawnmower on its highest blade height setting.

HARVEST

Harvest stems in early summer, just before or just as the plant begins to flower. To dry, hang tied bunches upside down somewhere dry and warm.

USES

Sweet woodruff is predominantly grown for its wonderful fragrance. The scent of the leaves gets stronger when dried, when it smells like freshly cut hay, with nutty vanilla elements. As a result it is used for scented wardrobe sachets, potpourri, and herb pillows. It was once used to stuff mattresses, hence its other common name of sweet-scented bedstraw. It is also used in Germany for flavoring drinks such as Maibowle, or May wine punch, as well as fruit salads, set desserts like jellies, syrups, and tea.

Drying sweet woodruff intensifies its fragrance.

CURRY PLANT
HELICHRYSUM ITALICUM

Curry plant is an evergreen subshrub or woody perennial that creates mounds of striking silver foliage, offering structure in the garden all year round. The narrow leaves have an intense curry aroma and are joined in summer by domed clusters of small, bright-yellow, button-like flowers.

PLANT TYPE Evergreen subshrub
HARDINESS Fully hardy, half-hardy
HEIGHT Up to 24 in (60 cm)
SPREAD Up to 31 in (80 cm)
SOIL Any well-drained soil except acid clay
LIGHT ☼

The **golden flowers** of curry plant add a decorative feature.

GROW AND MAINTAIN

As the name suggests, curry plant, *Helichrysum italicum*, has curry-scented foliage, but it should not be confused with curry leaf (see p.102), the plant usually used to impart that flavor in cooking. The cultivar 'Korma' has almost white stems and leaves. 'Dartington' is a more compact variety, growing to around 18 in (45 cm), with smaller leaves.

Curry plant is relatively hardy, but can be damaged by frost in cold areas; however, it is wet or damp conditions that usually cause the biggest problem in winter. Grow in a dry, sheltered spot in full sun, in poor to moderately fertile, well-drained soil. Avoid planting in heavy, wet, very acidic soil or exposed locations. It will grow well in containers given good drainage.

The best idea for beginners is to buy plants or use rooted cuttings. It is not that easy to grow from seed but you can try starting seeds off indoors in early spring in pots of seed starting mix, transplanting outside once all risk of frost has passed, or sow directly where it is to grow in late spring.

In colder climates, protect plants with a thick mulch over winter. Provide extra protection such as a cloche or horticultural fleece if the temperature drops below 14°F (–10°C).

PROPAGATE For best results, take softwood cuttings in spring, and semi-hardwood cuttings in the fall.

PRUNE Curry plant can grow leggy and bare toward the base if left to grow and flower freely. Prune in spring, cutting right back to within one or two leaves or buds of the previous year's growth. If growing for foliage only, nip off flowers when you see them. However, if you do wish to allow it to bloom, trim back the whole plant all over after flowering to retain a compact shape.

USES

Curry plant sprigs can be added to baked and roasted dishes, but the plant only imparts a mild curry flavor when cooked. The flowers can be used to make a herbal tea. It is more often used to be dried for its fragrance, in potpourri for instance, and for scented wreaths and flower arrangements.

HARVEST

Pick leaves for the kitchen any time, but for drying it's best to use young growth produced before the plant flowers. Harvest flowers when they have opened fully.

Curry plant is often grown just for its attractive, silvery, evergreen foliage.

HOPS *HUMULUS LUPULUS*

Commonly called hops, the hop plant, also known as hop vine, is a vigorous climber with twining hollow stems covered in stiff, prickly hairs that help it cling to and climb its support. It has palmate, five-pointed leaves with toothed edges, and small green-yellow flowers.

PLANT TYPE Deciduous perennial
HARDINESS Fully hardy
HEIGHT Up to 20 ft (6 m)
SPREAD Up to 6½ ft (2 m)
SOIL Any well-drained soil
LIGHT ☀ ☀
WARNING! Stems and flowers can cause skin irritation so wear gloves when handling

The female hop flowers add a fruity, slightly bitter taste to beer.

GROW AND MAINTAIN

Humulus lupulus, the common hop, has separate male and female plants, with different flowers. Male flowers are tiny and grow in loose clusters, while female flowers—the ones most used—are fragrant and cone-shaped with layers of papery scales. Good cultivars include 'Magnum', which is popular among home brewers, and 'Fuggle', which has large flowers and good resistance to disease. 'Aureus', known as the golden hop, has yellow leaves and is often grown as an ornamental climber.

Grow hops on a support in a south- or west-facing location in part shade or full sun. They will grow in most moderately fertile soils except those that are waterlogged or very acidic.

Humulus lupulus **'Aureus'** makes a bright and ornamental garden climber.

Hops are difficult to germinate from seed, and it is impossible to tell if you are growing male or female plants until they flower after 2–3 years, so it is best to buy plants to grow. Plant unpotted bare root plants 12 in (30 cm) deep, in winter or early spring, or plant potted plants to the same depth as in the pot, in spring or early summer.

Space plants at least 36 in (90 cm) apart. Choose three main stems per plant. Run canes or string from the support or trellis to the plant base and encourage the three vines to grow up them to reach the main support. Make sure they are firmly attached. Water regularly to establish, and mulch with well-rotted compost in early spring. Plants can suffer from powdery mildew, but pruning will help reduce the risk.

PROPAGATE Divide mature plants by digging up in late winter or early spring, and cut or separate outer sections of the rhizome that have a bud or growing point at the end. Replant immediately.

PRUNE When planting, remove all but the three chosen stems, all suckers, and all side shoots and leaves on the bottom 3 ft (1 m). In late fall, trim stems to within 24 in (60 cm) of the base.

HARVEST

Hop flowers should be harvested around late summer to early fall. The cones are ready once they become a bit papery and aromatic. They should all be harvested within 10 days or so. Dry quickly in a food dehydrator or in the oven on a low temperature (no more than 140°F/60°C), or over several days on a drying screen somewhere dark and warm. Refrigerate or freeze in food storage bags, or store in airtight containers somewhere dark.

USES

The unfertilized female flowers of hops are used in beer-making. They lend an aroma and a welcome bitterness to beer, balancing out the malty sweet flavor, and help keep a foamy head. They are also used to make dried floral garlands, and for hop pillows to calm and aid sleep.

HYSSOP
HYSSOPUS OFFICINALIS

This aromatic, woody perennial bears upright stems lined with narrow, lance-shaped leaves and topped with spikes of blue, white, or pink flowers in late summer and early fall. A relative of mint, it has a similar scent and pungent flavor with a medicinal, camphor-like edge.

PLANT TYPE Semi-evergreen subshrub
HARDINESS Fully hardy
HEIGHT 30 in (75 cm)
SPREAD Up to 36 in (90 cm)
SOIL Light, well-drained soil
LIGHT ☼ ☼

The colorful flower spires of hyssop are decorative in garden borders.

GROW AND MAINTAIN

Hyssopus officinalis, common or blue hyssop, has violet-blue blooms and dark green leaves. It is compact in form, but has a spreading habit. Fragrant and low-maintenance, it is often used as edging or as a low hedge and attracts pollinators such as bees and butterflies. Other forms include the cultivar 'Roseus', which has pink flowers, and *H. officinalis* f. *albus*, with white flowers. A quite different plant is *Agastache*, the anise or giant hyssop, which is usually just grown as an ornamental.

Hyssop does best in a sunny situation in fertile, alkaline to neutral soil that is well-drained. It won't tolerate being waterlogged, especially winter wet, and won't thrive in heavy clay or acid soils.

Buy plants during the growing season, or grow from seed. Sow indoors in early spring, into trays, modules, or small pots of seed starting mix. Sow thinly, placing seeds just beneath the surface, and covering lightly. Shoots should appear in about two weeks. Transplant seedlings into the garden after all risk of frost has passed, once you have hardened them off. Space plants at least 12 in (30 cm) apart. You can also grow hyssop in large pots.

Water regularly while it establishes, but be aware that this plant prefers drier conditions in general, and allow it to almost dry out between waterings. Mulch to protect overwinter.

PROPAGATE Allow to self-sow or collect seed after flowering, when ripe, to store and sow the following spring. However, the sown seedlings of pink or white hyssop may not reliably produce

Hyssopus officinalis **'Roseus'** is an equally attractive rose-pink cultivar.

USES

Hyssop can be used fresh, dried, or frozen, and is valued for its scent and flavor. The flowers are used for perfume and essential oil, and when dried make a soothing tea with a sweetener such as honey. The foliage is strong-tasting, but small amounts impart an interesting, slightly sharp note to salads, as well as stuffings, soups, stews, and pies, and the sharpness helps balance oily fish and fatty meat dishes.

flowers of the same color as the parent, so to be certain, take softwood cuttings in early summer.

PRUNE Deadhead spent blooms to encourage more to form, or just cut back all the flower heads after the plants have flowered—unless you are collecting seed. Trim back and tidy up plants all over in early spring to keep them compact and bushy.

HARVEST

Leaves are best picked in the morning. Harvest them when young, before the plant flowers. Pick flowers once they have opened. Dry bunches of leaves or flowers upside down somewhere dry, dark, and cool. Alternatively, keep them fresh in a food storage bag in the fridge, or in the freezer.

BAY *LAURUS NOBILIS*

Bay is a slow-growing evergreen shrub or small tree, grown both for its ornamental looks and for the kitchen, thanks to its aromatic, dark-green, ovate, smooth but leathery leaves. It also produces small yellow flowers in spring and glossy black fruit on female plants in the fall.

PLANT TYPE Evergreen shrub
HARDINESS Fully hardy, half-hardy
HEIGHT Up to 23 ft (7.5 m) unless pruned
SPREAD Up to 10 ft (3 m)
SOIL Any fertile, moist but well-drained soil
LIGHT ☼ ☀

Female bay trees may produce black berrylike fruits.

GROW AND MAINTAIN

Laurus nobilis, known as sweet bay or bay laurel, has a naturally upright habit and conical form. However, it is often kept to around 3 ft (1 m) tall with regular pruning, or clipped into topiary shapes such as cones and standards. The cultivar 'Aurea' has golden foliage, while 'Undulata' has leaves that look crimped. *L. nobilis* f. *angustifolia*, willow-leaved bay, has narrower, slightly wavy leaves. 'Saratoga' is a more compact form.

Grow in full sun or partial shade, in any fertile, moist but well-drained soil that does not stay wet in winter. Bay can be grown in containers in enriched, well-drained potting mix, but whether in pots or in the ground, choose a sheltered situation protected from cold, drying winds. Mature, established plants growing in the ground are hardier than young plants or those grown in containers.

Buy potted plants and plant any time between spring and late summer, spaced at least 12 in (30 cm) apart. Water in well and keep the soil just moist while establishing, but don't overwater. Plants grown in pots should be watered regularly, and repotted every few years. Feed bay with general liquid fertilizer in spring and summer.

If temperatures fall below 23°F (−5°C), protect those growing outside with horticultural fleece, and bring pot-grown specimens under cover in an unheated greenhouse or conservatory. Those caught by cold winds and frost may suffer from yellow or brown damaged foliage tips or even

Willow-leaved bay has slimmer, wavy leaves and can be hardier than the species.

USES

Bay leaves can be used fresh or dried for flavoring many recipes, including soups, stocks, stews, casseroles, and savory pie fillings, and are a main ingredient in a *bouquet garni*. Snap or lightly crush the dried leaves to release the aroma and add to dishes while cooking. Remove leaves before serving.

whole leaves—simply remove them in spring. Watch out for any damage to leaves caused by aphids or other sap-sucking insects.

PROPAGATE The most reliable method is to take semi-hardwood (semi-ripe) cuttings in late summer.

PRUNE In spring, if necessary, remove any dead or diseased shoots and any leaves or stems damaged by frost. Also take out any weak, wayward, crossing or rubbing, and inward-growing shoots, and cut any overlong shoots back to a healthy leaf node further down to keep the form neat and compact.

HARVEST

Pick leaves from established plants at any time of year. Dry by hanging upside down or laying on parchment paper somewhere dry and warm for a couple of weeks.

Bay trees are easily clipped into balls and other geometric topiary shapes.

LAVENDER *LAVANDULA*

Lavender is a low-maintenance, mounding shrub with aromatic gray-green foliage and highly scented blooms from late spring through summer. These fragrant flower spikes come in shades of blue and purple, but also occasionally pink and white, and are very appealing to pollinators.

PLANT TYPE Evergreen subshrub
HARDINESS Fully hardy, half-hardy
HEIGHT Up to 3 ft (1 m)
SPREAD Up to 4 ft (1.2 m)
SOIL Light or poor, very well-drained soil
LIGHT ☼

GROW AND MAINTAIN

There are several different types of lavender, such as English lavender, French or Spanish lavender, and lavandin. Hardy species include English lavender (*Lavandula angustifolia*) and its popular cultivars 'Munstead' and 'Hidcote', which flower in mid- and late summer. Taller-growing hybrid lavandin, *L. × intermedia*, and its varieties such as 'Grosso', 'Provence', and 'Seal' are also fully hardy, and bloom from early summer. These hardy types are the ones used most often commercially for scented cosmetics, as they produce the most fragrant oil.

'Munstead' is a popular, richly colored cultivar of English lavender.

Bees and other pollinators are particularly attracted to lavender.

The less hardy types—those that can't withstand temperatures below about 23°F (−5°C)—include *L. stoechas*, often called French, Spanish, or butterfly lavender, which has petal "ears" at the top of each flower, and is a much more compact plant with dark purple flowers. Cultivars include 'Kew Red', with flowers of deep red and pale pink.

Half-hardy species such as fringed lavender, *L. dentata*, won't survive below 32°F (0°C). It has toothed leaves and blooms over a long period in summer but is not as fragrant as other lavenders. It should be given a sheltered position or, in cooler climates, grown in pots, which can be brought inside over winter.

Lavandin 'Seal' has an extremely powerful fragrance.

Lavender is originally from the Mediterranean region and so is naturally drought-tolerant, and loves it hot and sunny. It hates wet conditions, especially in winter, and prefers a poor, sandy or chalky, well-drained soil that is neutral to alkaline. It will not perform well and may die in heavy, damp, clay soils, especially in cold and shady spaces.

Buy potted plants in spring and plant out once all risk of frost has passed. Choose a sheltered situation—for example, at the base of a south- or west-facing wall. Prepare the planting area and dig a hole large enough to accommodate the root ball, adding well-rotted compost or sand to the

Massed planting of lavender makes beautiful border edgings or hedges.

planting hole to improve drainage if necessary. Place the lavender at the same surface level as it was in the pot, backfill, and firm in gently with your hands. Space plants at least 36 in (90 cm) apart for individual plants. To make a lavender row, edging, or hedge, plant closer at 12–18 in (30–45 cm) apart. Water in well and keep well watered while the plants establish, but stop in the fall and don't irrigate over winter.

Lavender can also be cultivated in containers, which means you can still grow it even if you have heavy or wet soil and are in a cold climate. Use large pots and commercial citrus potting mix, enriched with compost, and perlite for drainage. Plants in pots will need to be watered more often.

Plants in the ground will benefit from a layer of mulch over winter. Bring pot-grown, less hardy types under cover, or wrap in bubble wrap or horticultural fleece if frost is forecast.

Watch out for leaves being eaten by shiny, multicolored rosemary beetles, and remove the insects by hand if seen. Lavender may get root rot in cold, damp ground or when overwatered.

PROPAGATE Take softwood cuttings in spring, or semi-hardwood cuttings in late summer or early fall.

PRUNE Cut back lavender every year to keep it dense and compact, and to stop it getting leggy. The number one rule for pruning any lavender is not to cut into old wood, because this causes damage, and the plant is unlikely to put on any new growth. On English lavender and lavandin, after flowering, trim back stems by at least one third or, on established plants, up to two thirds; just make sure you cut above where the lowest three or four new buds are developing on the stem. Give plants another light trim all over in spring if necessary. French or Spanish lavenders can be trimmed lightly all over after flowering finishes, leaving at least ¾ in (2 cm) of the current year's growth.

HARVEST

Pick the flowers just as the buds begin to open. To dry, hang small bunches upside down somewhere warm and dry for a couple of weeks.

'Kew Red' is a striking cultivar with two-tone flower heads.

USES

Lavender is beloved for its heady floral scent, which is a staple of the perfume and cosmetic industries. Home growers can use it dried for scented drawer and moth repellent sachets, for potpourri or air freshener, and in homemade soap or bath bombs. The fragrance is said to soothe, calm, and encourage sleep, so it is often used for herb pillows or bedside posies. Lavender has a very strong taste, so is used fresh quite sparingly in the kitchen, but is popular as a flavor in recipes such as shortbread and ice cream.

Filling the air with scent, lavender bunches are hung up to dry.

LOVAGE *LEVISTICUM OFFICINALE*

Little known but invaluable, lovage is tall and bushy with divided green leaves, like flat-leaf parsley but bigger, and yellow-green flowers in summer. It has a strong flavor similar to celery, with a hint of spice, and is one of the first herbs ready for picking in spring.

PLANT TYPE Deciduous perennial
HARDINESS Hardy
HEIGHT Up to 6½ ft (2 m)
SPREAD Up to 3 ft (1 m)
SOIL Fertile, moist, well-drained soil
LIGHT ☼ ☼
WARNING! May be toxic to cats

The fresh green leaves of lovage are tastiest picked when young.

Lovage seeds are produced in yellow, umbrella-shaped flower clusters.

GROW AND MAINTAIN

Also called smellage and sea parsley, *Levisticum officinale* is a pretty perennial herb that gets quite tall and so needs a position where it can have some space. It develops a long taproot and prefers a deep, rich soil that is moist but well-drained, in full sun or part shade. You may need to improve the soil by adding well-rotted manure or compost.

Sow seeds very thinly (you only need one or at most two plants) under cover in early spring into a tray or small pot of seed starting mix. Place in a heated propagator to germinate and remove the lid once shoots appear. When the seedlings are large enough to handle, prick out into individual pots and grow on. In late spring or early summer, after all risk of frost has passed, harden plants off for 10–14 days, before planting out in their final position. Alternatively, sow seed direct where they are to grow in fall, or buy pot-grown plants in spring. Space plants at least 24 in (60 cm) apart. You can also grow lovage in large containers.

Keep plants well watered throughout the growing season. Trim back all over in summer to promote a fresh flush of growth and keep a constant supply of tasty young foliage. When plants die back in the fall, cut leaves and foliage down to near the base.

Watch out for foliage damage from insect larvae—if seen, remove affected leaves and destroy them.

PROPAGATE Lovage will self-sow vigorously and so the simplest way to get more plants for free is to keep some of the seedlings and weed out the rest. Don't let your plants flower and set seed if you don't want them to spread. You can also collect seed and sow direct in the fall. Mature plants can also be divided in spring.

HARVEST

Pick or cut leaves and stalks, from the outside of the plant in, as needed from late spring until late summer. The best flavor is in young growth, before flowering. Leaves can also be dried, or frozen in ice cubes. To harvest seeds, allow plants to flower and snip off seed heads into paper bags, hanging upside to dry in a warm, well-ventilated, dark spot for a couple of weeks. Shake dried seeds into bags and store in an airtight container. Dig up roots in winter in the plant's second or third year.

USES

Lovage is very versatile in the kitchen but has a strong taste, so add sparingly. Young leaves are used for flavoring and garnish in soups and salads, and are good thinly shredded in mashed potatoes, scrambled eggs, and carrot and apple coleslaw. Stems can be steamed or candied, and roots can be cooked like any root vegetable. Seeds are used like celery seeds in dishes, and in bread and crackers.

BEE BALM *MELISSA OFFICINALIS*

A vigorous, easy-to-grow and low-maintenance perennial, bee balm is grown for its foliage—wrinkly, tooth-edged, oval, green leaves with a very strong lemony aroma. It also produces spires of small white or light yellow flowers in summer, which are a real magnet for bees.

PLANT TYPE Deciduous perennial
HARDINESS Hardy
HEIGHT Up to 32 in (80 cm)
SPREAD Up to 18 in (45 cm)
SOIL Any well-drained soil
LIGHT ☼ ☀
WARNING! May cause contact irritation for those with sensitive skin—wear gloves when handling

GROW AND MAINTAIN

Also known as lemon balm or sweet balm, *Melissa officinalis* is hardy and highly scented, with light green leaves. The cultivar 'All Gold' has bright yellow leaves, and does better in part shade, so the leaves don't get scorched in the summer sun. It is not as hardy as the species, so give it a sheltered spot and offer extra protection in winter such as mulch or horticultural fleece if the temperature drops below 23°F (–5°C).

Bee balm will thrive in a pot as long as it is kept well watered.

M. officinalis **'Aurea'** has bright and decorative variegated foliage.

The variegated variety called 'Aurea' has green and yellow-splashed leaves. For the best coloring, cut it back in early summer and then keep cutting it back regularly to promote fresh growth of young variegated leaves—otherwise it may revert and grow plain green leaves. There is also another cultivar called 'Compacta', which grows to just 6 in (15 cm) and is sterile, so won't spread via self-seeding like other bee balms.

Bee balm is not fussy and will grow happily in most situations, but likes full sun and well-drained soil, and hates winter wet.

Cultivars of this herb won't grow from seed and should be bought as ready-grown plants, but you can sow seed of the species in early spring under cover. Start off in trays or pots of seed starting mix and water lightly, placing in a heated propagator to germinate. Once they are large enough to handle, prick out seedlings and pot them up individually to grow on. Harden them off and then transplant into the garden where they are to grow.

USES

Fresh leaves make a famously soothing tea. As the scent is even stronger than the flavor, bee balm makes a powerful essential oil, and is used in homemade beeswax furniture polish, cosmetics such as lotions, bath salts, and home fragrance including potpourri and herb pillows. However, the leaves are also used in the kitchen to brighten up desserts and drinks, as well as to flavor savory dishes.

Plants should be spaced at least 12 in (30 cm) apart. Bee balm will also grow well in containers of enriched potting mix. Keep well watered while plants establish and during dry periods.

Take off flowers as they appear or deadhead to prevent self-sowing. Cut the plants back after flowering to encourage fresh growth. Look out for leaf-mottling damage from leafhoppers.

PROPAGATE Bee balm will self-sow freely. For named varieties, divide large clumps in spring or fall, or take softwood cuttings in spring or summer.

HARVEST

Pick leaves any time during the growing season—young leaves have the best scent and flavor before flowering. Leaves can be dried or frozen.

MINT *MENTHA*

A hardy, tough, and vigorous herb, mint is grown all over the world for its green leaves, which have a strong, fresh scent and taste that creates a cooling sensation in the mouth. This makes it the perfect flavoring for breath-freshening products like toothpaste and chewing gum.

PLANT TYPE Deciduous perennial
HARDINESS Fully hardy
HEIGHT Up to 24 in (60 cm)
SPREAD Indefinite
SOIL Any moist, well-drained soil
LIGHT ☼ ☼

GROW AND MAINTAIN

There are lots of different types of mint, with diverse scents and flavors of varying levels of intensity. Some are better than others for use in the kitchen. The best all-rounder is spearmint or garden mint, *Mentha spicata*, which is commonly available, easy to grow, and versatile, with good flavor. You can recognize it from its pointed leaves. The cultivar 'Tashkent' is recommended, as is Moroccan mint, *M. spicata* var. *crispa* 'Moroccan', the top choice for tea and drinks like cocktails, as it has the most intense flavor. Peppermint, *M. × piperita*, is strong in taste with a pungent aroma, and is the most widely sold.

Then there are mints with more unusual aromas and tastes, such as spicy ginger mint, *M. × gracilis*, and Eau de

Spearmint has a good flavor and is easy to grow.

Moroccan mint has a strong flavor and pretty, pale lilac flowers in summer.

Cologne mint, *M. × piperita* f. *citrata*, which smells like a mix of citrus and cologne—this one is best used for scent and not for flavor. Two of the most popular are apple mint, *M. suaveolens*, with its soft leaves, subtle flavor, and fresh apple-like fragrance, and *M. × piperita* f. *citrata* 'Chocolate', chocolate mint, which has a dark-brown flush on its leaves and tastes a bit like mint chocolate. Occasionally you will find unusual, lesser-grown varieties with hints of other fruity flavors and scents, such as the cultivars 'Banana', 'Lime', 'Grapefruit', 'Strawberry', 'Orange', and 'Berries and Cream'.

The less vigorous pineapple mint, *M. suaveolens* 'Variegata', is striking for its cream and green leaves, as well as its fruity pineapple-like scent. Another

Chocolate mint makes a cool, tasty flavoring for sweet dishes.

attractive foliage effect is seen on curly mint, *M. spicata* var. *crispa*, which has crinkled, frilly leaves. Low-growing *M. requienii*, Corsican mint, can be used for ground cover or herb lawns in shade (*see pp. 24–25*).

Mint spreads so easily that it is not typically grown from seed. Buy small, young plants in spring and they will quickly grow larger. It can also be planted in the fall. Choose a situation in part shade or full sun in any fertile, moist but well-drained soil—preferably a spot where it can have its roots in the shade and its leaves in the sun. Mint is a rampant grower and can spread fast, so it's best to plant it in a confined space such as a small raised bed on its own, in a trough, or in containers. To keep it under control you can grow it in a bed in a pot with the bottom cut out so the roots don't get congested, sunk into the ground, with a rim of at least 2 in (5 cm) left sticking out of the soil. If you are brave enough to grow it unconstrained in the ground, space plants by at least 18 in (45 cm). Don't grow different types of mint close to each other, to retain the best flavor of each.

Water well, especially during hot dry spells, to ensure lush leafy growth. Feed with a high-nitrogen fertilizer after flowering. As rapid growers, the roots get congested in pots, so they need to be divided in half every fall, and repotted with fresh potting mix. Use pot feet to lift up containers and ensure good drainage over winter.

Watch out for damage from rust, showing as orange spots on leaves. Destroy affected plants—burn or throw away; do not compost—and

Mint needs regular watering to keep the foliage lush and green.

Mint is best grown in containers to prevent it becoming invasive.

avoid planting mint, tarragon, or chives there again. Also look out for and pick off the green or blue mint beetles and their larvae, which eat the leaves.

PROPAGATE Mint is easy to divide—simply tip the plant out of the pot and cut in half using a spade or knife. Alternatively, cut off some of the roots or runners and pot them up in any potting mix, about 1 in (2.5 cm) under the surface, and water.

PRUNE After flowering, cut top growth back to 2 in (5 cm) from the base of the plant. This will encourage a flush of fresh leaves. You can also cut back the whole plant to ground level in the fall, as it starts to die back for winter.

HARVEST

You can harvest leaves continually from late spring to fall, from just a few weeks after planting. Pick them before the plant flowers for the best flavor—picking regularly or cutting back the plant before it can flower will prolong harvesting for as long as possible, and plants will respond very quickly with new growth. Always pick a sprig from the top, snipping it off just above a growing shoot. Leaves taste best fresh but can also be chopped up and frozen in ice cubes, or dried.

Fresh mint is a delicious addition to a pitcher of sangria.

USES

Mint is famous for its use in tea, which is purported to ease bloating and stomach discomfort. It is delicious in pea and mint soup; with butter on new potatoes; with feta in Greek salad; in Middle Eastern salads such as tabbouleh; and in mint sauce, used with lamb dishes. As well as this it brings pep to desserts like fruit salads, ice cream, and cakes, and in a cocktails such as mojitos, mint julep, or sangria.

Pineapple mint has attractive variegated foliage.

CURRY LEAF *MURRAYA KOENIGII*

Curry leaf is a subtropical evergreen shrub or small tree, with aromatic pinnate leaves that are made up of many ovate green leaflets. As the name suggests, the foliage gives the scent and flavor of curry. This plant also has small white star-shaped flowers and dark fruits.

PLANT TYPE Evergreen or semi-evergreen shrub
HARDINESS Tender
HEIGHT Up to 20 ft (6 m)
SPREAD Up to 16 ft (5 m)
SOIL Light, well-drained soil
LIGHT ☀ ☀

Curry leaves grow in an attractive pattern of alternating pairs of leaflets.

Dark purple-black berries can be produced if the curry leaf plant blooms.

GROW AND MAINTAIN

Also known as sweet neem, *Murraya koenigii* is tender, and is often grown indoors as a houseplant or under glass in a greenhouse or conservatory. If grown in a container, it can be placed outdoors in a sheltered position during hot, sunny weather in summer.

Plants are available from specialized nurseries and, although they are small and slow-growing, they will eventually grow into small trees, and even indoors in a pot they may reach a height of around 5 ft (1.5 m).

Grow in a container only slightly larger than the plant's root ball, repotting in spring or summer as the plant grows larger. Use commercial citrus mix with added compost and perlite for drainage. Place in a light, warm position, such as a bright windowsill, away from drying heat sources like vents or cold drafts, keeping the plant at a temperature of 64–68°F

(18–20°C). Water well and let it drain (don't leave it sitting in water), and allow the soil to dry out between waterings.

In summer, feed with citrus plant fertilizer according to the instructions on the label. In the winter, keep the temperature above 59°F (15°C). In low light levels and cooler temperatures, the plant, although evergreen, may act as a semi-evergreen and lose some or all of its leaves. Water only rarely over the winter and don't feed. In spring, start to water more often, and growth will begin again.

Look out for leaf damage caused by aphids and other insects. Most pests can be kept under control by washing leaves with horticultural soap.

PROPAGATE If your plant fruits, you can remove the berrylike flesh to get to the seed inside. Sow when ripe, in fall, into plugs or pots of seed starting mix, and place in a heated propagator. Be aware that you could wait around three

months or more for seeds to germinate. It may be more successful to take semi-hardwood cuttings in early summer. Some plants may produce suckers at the base, which can be removed and potted up.

HARVEST

You can begin to pick leaves once your new plants put on some growth—typically in summer in cooler climates. Keep picking regularly to encourage fresh growth. The leaves are best fresh but they can be dried or frozen.

USES

Curry leaf is used widely in Indian cooking, especially to flavor soups and curries. Leaves are used whole, either added to sauces or fried in oil at the beginning of cooking to impart the taste.

Fried curry leaves add extra spice to a mango soup.

SWEET CICELY *MYRRHIS ODORATA*

A beautiful upright plant that is one of the first herbs to come into leaf and flower in spring, sweet cicely has deeply divided, fernlike foliage with a sweet but aniseed scent and flavor. The white blooms are pretty and attractive to bees and other pollinators.

PLANT TYPE Deciduous perennial
HARDINESS Hardy
HEIGHT Up to 3 ft (1 m)
SPREAD Up to 24 in (60 cm)
SOIL Any well-drained soil
LIGHT ☀

Sweet cicely's flowers have a sugary scent, and brighten a shady woodland planting.

USES

Sweet cicely leaves have been traditionally used to partially replace sugar in recipes, so less sugar is needed to sweeten tart fruit, for example. They are also used to make tea, as well as to add an anise taste to savory dishes like soups, stews, salads, and egg and fish dishes. Crushed seeds will add a nutty flavor to fruit salads, baked pastry and cakes, and ice cream. The root is used as a vegetable, cooked or raw, and to make wine.

GROW AND MAINTAIN

Myrrhis odorata has feathery green leaves in spring and flat clusters of tiny white blooms in late spring or early summer. It is very hardy, emerging early in the season and continuing to grow well into the fall.

Grow in any well-drained soil. It will tolerate a variety of conditions including poor or heavy clay soils perfectly well, but prefers a light and fertile soil—though be aware it can spread easily in ideal conditions. Sweet cicely likes it cool, not hot, so part shade is best.

Start from seed, which needs a period of cold to germinate. As a result, it is best to sow outside in the fall, where it is to grow, so it will experience winter temperatures and is encouraged to sprout the following spring when things begin to warm up. Alternatively, sow one seed each into plugs or small pots of seed starting mix and leave out over winter. You could also start in spring if you first place the seed in a small bag of sand in the refrigerator for several weeks before sowing. Once they are large enough to handle, thin out or transplant resulting seedlings to 24 in (60 cm) apart in the garden. Sweet cicely develops a long taproot, and so is not suitable for growing in containers.

Keep plants well watered while they establish. Cut down spent flower stalks to encourage fresh growth and prevent self-sowing. For fresh growth, trim back the whole plant after flowering. Mulch with well-rotted manure or garden compost in the fall. Remove dead foliage and stalks once the plant has died back for winter.

PROPAGATE Sweet cicely will self-sow and spread easily and rapidly around where it is originally grown, or you can collect the seed after flowering and sow it ripe in the fall. You can also divide plants in the fall, or take root cuttings. Dig up the tap root and cut into sections, each with a shoot or bud attached, and replant.

HARVEST

Pick leaves as you need them from spring onward. Seeds can be collected as they begin to ripen, in summer and fall, by snipping off seed heads as they turn brown. Shake or rub out seeds from the seed capsules into a paper bag, and store them in an airtight container. One-year-old roots can be dug up in the fall.

CATMINT *NEPETA*

Catmint has toothed, gray-green, aromatic foliage with a spicy, fresh but faintly musky scent, like a complex mix of mint, cloves, and sage. It produces spikes of purple-blue, pink, or white blooms over a long period from late spring through summer, which are highly attractive to pollinators.

PLANT TYPE Deciduous perennial
HARDINESS Fully hardy
HEIGHT Up to 36 in (90 cm)
SPREAD Up to 24 in (60 cm)
SOIL Any well-drained soil
LIGHT ☼ ☼

Nepeta racemosa **'Snowflake'** has pretty white to creamy-white flowers.

GROW AND MAINTAIN

Beautiful, tough, and easy to grow, catmint is so named because cats love eating and rubbing up against the plant, drawn by the scent. The most widely sold garden cultivar is the largest, *Nepeta* 'Six Hills Giant', which reaches 36 in (90 cm) high and bears a mass of upright spires smothered in small purple flowers, from late spring or early summer all the way through the growing season.

N. racemosa 'Walker's Low' is also very popular, and looks similar, with masses of blue-mauve blooms, but it tends to be more compact, growing to about 24–32 in (60–80 cm). The variety 'Snowflake' has white flowers. *N. × faassenii* is smaller, growing to 18–24 in (45–60 cm) with pretty lavender-blue blooms, and its cultivar 'Kit Kat' (also sold as 'Kit Cat') is the most compact at just 12 in (30 cm). Another worthwhile type to look out for is *N. subsessilis* 'Sweet Dreams', which has pink flowers and can cope with moister soil than other catmints.

Cats like catmint generally, but the true catnip is *N. cataria*, which has purple-spotted white flowers later in the season, from summer into fall.

Grow in a sunny spot for best results, or light shade. Catmint will tolerate a wide range of soil types, as long as it is well-drained, but does not do well in waterlogged or heavy soils like clay and may rot off in the ground in a wet winter.

For catmints that can be grown from seed (many cultivars are sterile), sow direct in spring, into the ground where they are to grow or into pots or trays of seed starting mix. Thin out seedlings once they are large enough to handle. Alternatively, buy pot-grown plants and plant in spring or fall, or at any time during the growing season as long as you can water them regularly while they establish. Depending on the cultivar and its eventual spread, plants should be spaced 8–24 in (20–60 cm) apart. Compact catmints can also be grown in containers.

These plants are low maintenance: there is no need to feed them, and once established they are fairly drought-tolerant. If the floppy habit of some larger forms is a problem they can be staked. Deadhead spent blooms to encourage more flowers.

USES

Catmint, fresh or dry, can be added to dishes for a spicy, slightly minty taste, and used to make tea. It is also a source of utter bliss for cats, stuffed fresh or dried in toys for them to play with and enjoy. It makes a beautiful ornamental garden plant to edge a path or in borders with other perennials.

Cats love to play with toys stuffed with catmint.

Catmints like 'Walker's Low' are attractive both to butterflies and other pollinators, and in the border.

Catmint is generally pest-free, and is deer-resistant, but can suffer from powdery mildew. The main problem (or benefit, depending on your viewpoint) is that many cats in the vicinity will be drawn to it and will eat, loll about all over, and flatten the plant. Some gardeners have found that inserting twiggy branches in and around the plant can keep them off or at least limit the damage.

PROPAGATE Divide established plants in spring, or take softwood cuttings in early summer.

PRUNE Catmint can be sprawling, billowing, bushy plants and should be cut back by half after flowering to neaten the form and produce a second flush of growth. Alternatively, cut back by a third in May to encourage more compact growth; or pinch out the tips to promote a bushier habit.

HARVEST

Harvest leaves when young, and flowers as they begin to bloom. Use fresh or dry upside down or on a rack, and store in an airtight container.

True catnip, *Nepeta cataria*, is irresistible to most cats.

BASIL *OCIMUM*

Encompassing the sweeter varieties used in Italian cooking, the more aniseed-like Thai basil, and even vividly colorful varieties, basil is a short-lived herb with luscious, very fragrant leaves that have a warm, peppery taste. Spikes of small flowers appear in late summer.

PLANT TYPE Deciduous annual
HARDINESS Tender
HEIGHT Up to 20 in (50 cm)
SPREAD Up to 12 in (30 cm)
SOIL Light, well-drained soil
LIGHT ☼

The fresh green leaves of sweet basil release an intense aroma when crushed.

GROW AND MAINTAIN

Ocimum basilicum, sweet basil, is the most widely grown and used basil and has large green leaves and white flowers. One of the best to grow for the kitchen is 'Sweet Green', with a spicy, clove-like aroma; another is 'Genovese', which has a richer, deeper flavor and fragrance than the species. The cultivar 'Horapha', Thai basil, has a stronger licorice taste and is used in Asian cuisine. 'Cinnamon', with its dark green-brown leaves and purple stems, has an intense, sweet, cinnamon aroma.

Purple or dark opal basil, *O. basilicum* var. *purpurascens,* is highly scented with dark purple foliage, and reaches around 12 in (30 cm). The cultivar 'Purple Ruffles' has larger, wavy-edged leaves and pink flowers. *O. minimum* 'Greek', known as Greek or bush basil, has small green leaves with a more subtle flavor.

Lemon basil, *O. × citriodorum*, has yellow-washed, toothed leaves and a lovely citrus aroma and taste. Other interesting types for appearance or taste include lime basil; lettuce-leaved basil; camphor basil; and *O. tenuiflorum,* holy basil, much used in herbal medicine. An unusual choice is African basil, a rare perennial, but its clove scent and flavor is so strong that it is hardly ever used in cooking.

Grow in a light, sandy or loamy, moderately fertile, well-drained soil in a really sunny, sheltered spot. Basil hates cold, wet soil and loves heat—it is frost-tender and will blacken and die in temperatures below around 41°F (5°C). It can also be grown in pots, outdoors or inside on a sunny windowsill.

Sow seed under cover in early spring, scattering thinly into pots or cell trays of moist seed starting mix. Cover lightly and firm in. Ideally, place in a heated

propagator, or put somewhere warm and bright. Take out of the propagator once shoots show. When seedlings are large enough to handle, thin out those growing in small pots to one per pot, or pot on cell tray plugs into larger individual pots. Grow on indoors until after all risk of frost.

Watch out for a fungal disease called damping off, which kills seedlings: prevent attacks by keeping them warm and in a dry atmosphere with good airflow. Don't overwater and, when you water, do it early in the day, from the bottom (sitting the pot in water for a few minutes rather than wetting the top of the plant). Harden plants off for 10–14 days, moving them outside in the day and back in at night, before planting out in their final location.

You can also sow seed direct into the ground or a pot of potting mix, or buy young plants and plant out in late spring

Thai basil has a strong taste and attractive, red-tinted leaves and flowers.

Cinnamon basil has striking dark stems and leaves that have a sweet flavor.

Purple basil has richly colored leaves with a highly perfumed scent.

Greek basil has small leaves and a mild taste and makes a compact, bushy plant.

Basil leaves should be torn to release the flavor, and added at the end of cooking. Basil is a staple of Italian cuisine, used liberally in sauces for pasta, with fresh tomato and mozzarella in a caprese salad, to top pizzas, and as the star of pesto sauce and the French *sauce au pistou*. Thai basil is used in Southeast Asian curries, spring rolls, and savory noodle dishes.

Basil is also excellent for making flavored oil and vinegar and other salad dressings. It makes an unusual but tasty flavor for ice cream, and a dessert with strawberries, black pepper, and balsamic vinegar.

Basil's strong scent seems to repel insects. Many gardeners keep a pot by windows and outdoor dining areas, and also grow it alongside tomatoes, as a companion plant.

after all risk of frost has passed. Space the plants 8–16 in (20–40 cm) apart, depending on the variety. Repeat sow every few weeks if you want to ensure a continuous supply.

Keep plants well watered in summer, but always water in the morning and avoid splashing leaves to prevent attack from another fungal disease, powdery mildew. Also watch out for aphids, and damage from slugs and snails.

Pinch out the tips of the young plants to promote bushy growth and prevent flowering. Remove any flowers that start to appear because the leaf flavor will be more bitter once the plant begins to bloom.

PROPAGATE Allow plants to flower and develop seed heads, then collect the seed and sow the following season.

HARVEST

Basil can be ready for harvesting from about 2 months after planting. Harvest regularly, picking off leaves as you need them or, preferably, pinching or cutting off stems at just above where a pair of leaves are showing, which will also encourage bushy growth. Always pick from the top. Make sure to harvest anything usable left on the plant toward the start of fall, before the first frost.

Use leaves immediately or pop stems in a glass or vase of water at room temperature, as you would a bouquet. This is the easiest way to keep leaves fresh for a few days. They will quickly wilt and may go black or brown in the

Classic pesto sauce is made with basil, pine nuts, garlic, and Parmesan.

Pinch out basil stems just above a pair of leaves to make bushy plants.

fridge, if bruised or damp and stored in plastic, unless a huge amount of care is taken with them.

For long-term storage, leaves are best blitzed in oil and then frozen in ice cube trays. They can also be dried and kept in an airtight container, but it is difficult to do this properly at home, and the flavor doesn't keep as well.

OREGANO/MARJORAM

ORIGANUM

Origanum species typically have aromatic, ovate, green, and somewhat hairy foliage and clusters of pink, pale purple, or white summer flowers that are a magnet for bees. The scents and flavors of the leaves vary in profile and intensity from subtle, sweet, and woody to earthy, strong, and spicy.

PLANT TYPE Deciduous perennial
HARDINESS Fully hardy, half-hardy
HEIGHT Up to 18 in (45 cm)
SPREAD Up to 18 in (45 cm)
SOIL Any light, well-drained soil
LIGHT ☼

GROW AND MAINTAIN

Origanum originates from the mountains of the Mediterranean and Middle East, but now a broad range of species and varieties with diverse characteristics grow all over the world. Some are low and mounding, while others are tall and upright. The common names oregano and marjoram are often, confusingly, applied to all or various plants in the genus. In Mexico, a completely different plant, *Lippia*, is known as oregano.

Origanum vulgare, called wild marjoram or common oregano, is widespread, hardy, and variable from

Common oregano, or wild marjoram, has attractive, pollinator-friendly flowers.

Golden oregano is a compact cultivar with bright foliage.

plant to plant, but generally has large leaves, mauve flowers, and a strong flavor. Greek oregano, *O. vulgare* subsp. *hirtum* 'Greek', is even stronger-flavored, and is the cultivated type most commonly grown for and used in the kitchen. Golden oregano, *O. vulgare* 'Aureum', has yellow foliage and pale purple blooms. 'Nanum' is a dwarf cultivar at just 8 in (20 cm) with tiny leaves and white or pale pink flowers.

Another popular type is pot marjoram, *Origanum onites*, which has small, dark green leaves and mauve-pink

Pot marjoram has delicate clusters of pink or mauve flowers in late summer.

flowers. It is not as hardy as common oregano so will appreciate a sheltered spot in the garden.

The plant known as sweet marjoram or knotted marjoram, *O. majorana*, has a sweeter and more floral aroma, with pale green leaves and white flowers. It is only half hardy, so although it is perennial it is often grown as an annual in colder climates.

There are also ornamental oreganos like *O. laevigatum* 'Herrenhausen', 'Kent Beauty', and 'Hopley's'. Their leaves are milder-tasting, and although they will

Slightly tender sweet marjoram has small, rounded leaves that have a delicate, floral fragrance.

impart flavor in cooking, they are usually grown more for the appearance of their foliage and flowers, and, like their culinary cousins, are a huge draw for bees and other pollinating insects.

Origanum likes warm and dry conditions, and doesn't mind poor soil. Grow in a sunny spot, preferably in light or sandy, well-drained soil. Avoid planting in wet, heavy clay, or very acidic soils.

The species and cultivars that can be guaranteed to come true when grown from seed are common oregano, sweet marjoram, and Greek oregano. Sow these under cover in spring, very thinly, onto the surface of pots or trays of seed starting mix. Water gently, and germinate if possible in a heated propagator with the lid off. Thin out to a few strong seedlings per pot, and then prick out into individual small pots once large enough to handle. Harden off and transplant outside to their final growing position once all risk of frost has passed. For the other types and cultivars, buy pot-grown plants in spring. Space plants 8–12 in (20–30 cm) apart, depending on the variety.

You may need to water when dry during the first season and if grown in containers, but in general these plants are quite drought-tolerant.

Origanum 'Kent Beauty' is usually grown for its intricate flowers.

PROPAGATE Not all *Origanum* types will come true from seed, meaning the sown seedlings won't match the characteristics of the parent plant. You can allow the three types named left to self-sow, or let the plants flower and set seed before collecting and storing to sow the following season. Most species and cultivars can be propagated via softwood cuttings in early summer. Common oregano can be divided in spring.

PRUNE Clip back plants after flowering to encourage fresh growth. Cut back all over to about 2 in (5 cm) from the base in the fall to keep a compact form, or cut back dead stems and neaten up in spring.

HARVEST

Harvest leaves as needed in summer before the flowers appear, picking leaves or snipping off sprigs. Dry stems by hanging upside down somewhere warm, dry, and dark for a couple of weeks. Strip off dried leaves and store in an airtight container.

USES

Oregano is widely used in Italian cooking, especially tomato sauces for pizzas and pastas, and for flavor in Tuscan panzanella bread salad with tomatoes. It is also common in Greek cooking, and in dressings and sauces such as Argentinian chimichurri. The leaves can be used whole or, as they can be fuzzy, chopped up small for a better mouth feel. Use whole fresh sprigs of sweet marjoram for baking with white fish in white wine and remove before serving. Dried oregano is used in *herbes de Provence* and also the Middle Eastern za'atar spice mix, with ground sumac and sesame seeds.

Fresh oregano leaves add intense flavor to home-cooked pizza.

SCENTED-LEAF GERANIUM *PELARGONIUM*

PLANT TYPE Evergreen perennial
HARDINESS Tender, half-hardy
HEIGHT Up to 24 in (60 cm)
SPREAD Up to 20 in (50 cm)
SOIL Fertile, well-drained soil
LIGHT ☼

Scented-leaf geraniums are grown for their highly fragrant, textured, often divided leaves, which release intense aromas when rubbed. The leaves may also be variegated or marked with interesting patterns.

GROW AND MAINTAIN

Although known as geraniums, these plants are not related to hardy border geraniums and are in fact a different genus—*Pelargonium*. They originated in South Africa, which means that they like warm conditions, and so in colder climates they are usually grown in pots placed outdoors for the summer and kept under cover in winter. They can also be grown as houseplants in a conservatory or greenhouse. Like the pelargoniums used for summer bedding, scented-leaf geraniums have pretty flowers, usually small and pink or white, which appear in summer.

One of the most widely known is *Pelargonium* 'Attar of Roses', with its strong rose scent, soft green leaves, and pink flowers. 'Sweet Mimosa' is another rose-scented cultivar. Lemon-scented types include 'Lemon Fancy'; 'Atomic Snowflake', which has variegated silver-green leaves; and the intensely fragrant 'Mabel Grey' with mauve-pink blooms. *P. crispum* 'Variegatum' is also lemon-scented, with crinkly variegated cream and green leaves, but is not recommended for using in the kitchen as it may irritate the stomach.

There is an enormous range of other varieties available with various scents, but some recommended cultivars

USES

While scented-leaf pelargoniums are used in aromatherapy oils and perfumery, the home gardener can use the leaves for potpourri, and in the kitchen for tea, and to infuse desserts and drinks with flavors. Use them to make a delicious sugar syrup to flavor ice creams, sorbets, jellies, jams, cocktails, and punch, or to line the pans of cakes and muffins (remove before eating). The flowers are edible and are often used to decorate desserts.

'Sweet Mimosa' has pink and dark-pink splattered flowers and a rose scent.

'Attar of Roses' offers a strong rose fragrance and pink flowers.

'Variegatum' has lemon-scented leaves with crinkled, creamy variegated edges.

'Mabel Grey' presents attractively painted pink and mauve flowers and leaves with a sharp lemon scent.

'Lilian Pottinger' has dainty white flowers and a spicy apple scent.

'Chocolate Peppermint' has handsomely patterned fragrant leaves.

include apple-scented 'Lilian Pottinger', orange-scented 'Prince of Orange', spice and pine-scented Fragrans Group, eucalyptus-scented 'Clorinda', and 'Chocolate Peppermint', which has beautiful brown-patterned green leaves that smell like its name.

Buy plants or plugs in spring, and grow on under cover somewhere warm and bright until all risk of frost has passed. They will do best in pots at least 6 in (15 cm) wide and deep, filled with a commercial potting mix with added compost and some extra perlite for drainage. Include some slow-release fertilizer. Harden plants off and place out in their final growing position, in full sun, somewhere you can reach out and touch the leaves or brush past them. Water regularly during summer. To encourage bushy growth, pinch out the growing tips in early summer. Deadhead spent flowers.

Before the first frosts, bring them under cover for the winter. Water only when the potting mix is completely dry. In spring, repot into a larger container if necessary. Begin watering more often to keep the soil moist and start to feed regularly with a general liquid fertilizer.

Alternatively, treat as an annual and discard plants at the end of the season, as the frost will kill them if they are left outdoors over winter.

Pelargoniums can be affected by rust and gray mold. Watch out for sap-sucking insects and remove them.

PROPAGATE Take softwood cuttings in summer.

PRUNE Trim back plants by about a third before bringing them indoors for the winter. Give another trim in spring if necessary to remove dead material and keep a compact shape.

HARVEST

Pick or snip off leaves throughout summer as needed.

SHISO *PERILLA FRUTESCENS*

Popular in East Asia, shiso is grown for its nettle-like, sometimes frilly leaves in green or purple, which have a cinnamon-like scent and a highly unusual flavor that is a mishmash of many spicy and herbal notes, including ginger, mint, clove, basil, and lemon.

PLANT TYPE Annual
HARDINESS Hardy
HEIGHT Up to 4 ft (1.2 m)
SPREAD Up to 24 in (60 cm)
SOIL Any well-drained soil
LIGHT ☼ ☼

GROW AND MAINTAIN

Also known as Japanese basil, beefsteak plant, and purple mint, amongst other names, shiso is hugely popular in the cuisine of countries such as Japan, China, and Korea, but was grown and known mostly as an ornamental annual in Western countries until recently. As a result, there is enduring confusion over the botanical names of the different types available.

Perilla frutescens, called green shiso or Korean perilla, or given the cultivar name 'Britton' by many seed sellers, is a bicolor type with tooth-edged green leaves with purple undersides, and small white summer flowers. *P. frutescens* var. *crispa* or var. *purpurascens*, known as red or purple shiso, has curly, crinkly-edged, purple-bronze foliage, and pink flowers. There is also a plain green version which many people also call green shiso.

Grow in any moderately fertile, well-drained soil, in full sun or part shade. You can buy pot-grown plants to plant out in spring, or start from seed. Some gardeners recommend soaking the seeds overnight in water before sowing to improve chances of germination. Sow under cover in early spring, onto the surface of plugs or small pots of seed starting mix, and place in a heated propagator to germinate. Pot on seedlings once they are large enough to handle, and harden off once all risk of frost has passed, so they can be planted out in the garden. Alternatively, sow outside where they are to grow in late spring. Space or thin plants to 12 in (30 cm) apart. Water in well and water during dry periods.

Shiso can also be grown in containers, as long as it is watered regularly and fed during the growing season with liquid fertilizer.

Pinch out growing tips to keep plants bushy and productive. In the fall, after the plants have died back, lift and discard on the compost heap.

PROPAGATE Allow plants to flower and collect seed from seed heads in the fall to store and sow the following spring.

USES

Green shiso is the one most often used in the kitchen, especially in Japanese cuisine, in tempura, salads, and stir-fries, and as a garnish for sushi. Purple shiso is used to color pickles like umeboshi salted plums, and as a microleaf by chefs.

HARVEST

Leaves may be ready for harvesting from as soon as two months after sowing, and can then be picked continuously all season.

Well-grown shiso seedlings are ready to plant out after hardening off.

Red shiso's beautiful purple coloring makes it ornamental as well as useful.

VIETNAMESE CORIANDER

PERSICARIA ODORATA

PLANT TYPE Evergreen perennial
HARDINESS Tender
HEIGHT 20–39 in (50–100 cm)
SPREAD 12 in (30 cm) or more
SOIL Moist, fertile, well-drained soil
LIGHT ☼ ☼

This tasty, tender herb has red stems and lance-shaped green leaves with maroon-brown markings near the base. The foliage smells like coriander, but stronger and more spicy, and has a peppery lime flavor that turns hot. It is vigorous, and often invasive in warm climates.

Vietnamese coriander leaves have striking and attractive markings.

GROW AND MAINTAIN

Also called Asian mint or rau ram, Vietnamese coriander is a tropical herb, previously classified as *Polygonum odoratum*. It won't survive outside below about 45–50°F (7–10°C), so in colder climates it is best to grow it in a pot indoors, in a greenhouse or conservatory or on a bright windowsill, and place it outside only in summer, in a warm, sheltered situation.

Buy pot-grown plants and plant in enriched potting mix in containers. Inside, place somewhere bright and light, but protect from drafts, direct afternoon sun through glass, and heating sources such as vents. When the temperature outside is high enough, you can move pots outdoors.

Keep plants well watered, and feed with liquid fertilizer in summer. Cut back in midsummer to encourage fresh growth. Bring inside before the first frosts, reduce watering, and don't feed over winter. Repot each year with fresh potting mix into a slightly larger pot, or divide regularly.

Alternatively, plant outside once the risk of frost has passed, in a sheltered, sunny spot in rich, moist but well-drained soil. Treat as an annual and lift and discard on the compost heap in fall, or pot up and bring indoors for winter.

PROPAGATE Divide in fall or spring. Take semi-ripe cuttings in late spring or summer, snipping off stems below a joint. Cuttings root easily.

HARVEST

Pick leaves throughout the growing season as required. In colder climates when grown indoors in a pot, it is best to harvest sparingly or hardly at all over winter, when growth slows down.

For use in cooking, Vietnamese coriander should be picked fresh and added at the end for best flavor.

USES

Vietnamese coriander is a favorite ingredient in Southeast Asian cuisine, particularly in Vietnamese pho and other noodle dishes, and is used in stir-fries, curries, and summer and spring rolls. Use fresh leaves and put them in at the end of the cooking time—the coriander-like fragrance dissipates if cooked for too long. Use the leaves sparingly at first until you find your preferred taste concentration, as they are strong and spicy.

PARSLEY *PETROSELINUM CRISPUM*

Parsley is grown for its rich green, divided, aromatic leaves, which can be flat or curled in form. The flavor is fresh and has a brightening effect like citrus, but tastes greener and more earthy. In its second year it produces flat clusters of small yellow-green flowers.

PLANT TYPE Semi-evergreen biennial
HARDINESS Hardy
HEIGHT Up to 18 in (45 cm)
SPREAD Up to 12 in (30 cm)
SOIL Fertile, moist but well-drained soil
LIGHT ☀ ☼

'Moss Curled' is a bushy, robust, curly parsley with a fine, grassy taste.

Flat-leaved or Italian parsley has a strong and aromatic flavor.

GROW AND MAINTAIN

Parsley is biennial, which means that in its first year it produces a rosette of leaves, and in its second it also bears flowers and sets seed in summer. The leaves are softer and more flavorful in its first season and so it is usually grown as an annual, with new plants sown each spring.

There are two main types of parsley. As its name suggests, curled-leaf parsley, *Petroselinum crispum*, has tooth-edged leaves that are scrunched up and crinkly. Good cultivars include 'Moss Curled' and 'Lisette'. *Petroselinum*

crispum var. *neapolitanum*, known variously as flat-leaved, broad-leaved, and Italian parsley, has a flat, divided leaf and is used more in the kitchen as it has a stronger and, many think, better flavor. It is often sold under the names 'Italian Giant' or 'French' parsley.

Grow in any fertile, moist but well-drained soil, preferably in part shade. The soil can be improved with well-rotted garden compost or manure in the fall. Parsley can also be grown in pots, outside or indoors on a bright windowsill. Sow seed under cover in spring into cell trays or small pots of seed starting mix. Parsley has a tap root

and hates to be disturbed, so it's best not to move it too often—for example, by sowing into trays and then having to prick out seedlings; disturbance like this can lead to bolting. Cover lightly and keep moist. Germination is erratic so don't lose heart if only some seeds sprout. Thin out seedlings once they are large enough to handle. Transplant carefully outside once all risk of frost has passed, after hardening plants off.

When planting out parsley try to disturb the roots as little as possible.

Remove some seedlings to give the remaining plants room to grow.

Parsley needs regular and plentiful watering to grow well.

Cut whole sprigs down to the ground when harvesting..

Alternatively, sow seed direct outdoors in late spring into prepared soil where the plants are to grow. Keep moist. Thin out or space plants to at least 6 in (15 cm) apart. Sow fresh seed every few weeks through spring and summer for a continual fresh supply.

Water regularly, especially during dry periods, to prevent bolting (running to flower). If it does start to bolt, remove the flower heads immediately. However, this may mean it is past its best already and has become bitter, so you should sow or plant replacements. Feed with a liquid general fertilizer through summer.

In the fall, to prolong the harvest, you can protect plants with a cloche, or pot up and bring inside to grow on through winter somewhere bright. Keep watering and feeding. If growing as an annual, lift and discard plants on the compost heap.

Watch out for damage from slugs and snails, and fungal disease.

PROPAGATE Allow the plant to flower and form seed heads, collect seed, and store in an airtight container until sowing the following season.

HARVEST

Leaves can be harvested from when there are eight or more leaves on the plant, all through the season. Pick leaves and sprigs regularly to encourage vigorous leafy growth. Use freshly cut, or pop stems into a jar of water at room temperature for a few days.

Stems with leaves will stay in good shape in a food storage bag in the fridge for up to two weeks. Drying saps all the flavor from parsley, so for long-term storage, freeze—either double-bagging bunches in sealed freezer bags (with as much air pushed out as possible) or chopping up leaves and freezing in water in ice-cube trays.

USES

Stalks of parsley can be added to dishes while they are cooking, for example as part of a *bouquet garni*, but leaves are usually added at the very end, just before serving, for the best flavor. Parsley is a ubiquitous garnish and adds flavor to soups, roasted meat and vegetable dishes, stuffing, and egg dishes like frittata or quiche. It is the main ingredient of tabbouleh salad, salsa verde, and gremolata, as well as in parsley sauce. It's a great match for dishes featuring lemons, mushrooms, or buttered new potatoes, and can be chewed to freshen the breath.

Chopped parsley brightens up a simple white sauce for fish.

SORREL *RUMEX*

Sorrel is an easy-to-grow perennial cultivated for its arrow-shaped green leaves, which have a tart, lemony tang. They are used as an herb, and sometimes also as a vegetable, like spinach, for salads and cooked dishes. If allowed, it will produce small green-brown flowers in summer.

PLANT TYPE Deciduous perennial
HARDINESS Hardy
HEIGHT 12–39 in (30 cm–100 cm)
SPREAD 12–24 in (30–60 cm) or more
SOIL Fertile, moist but well-drained soil
LIGHT ☼ ☼
WARNING! Toxic for pets—may cause stomach upset for cats and dogs if ingested, and in humans may cause contact irritation for sensitive skin

GROW AND MAINTAIN

There are several different plants called sorrel. Garden or common sorrel, *Rumex acetosa*, is also called broad-leaved sorrel. The most popular for use in the kitchen is buckler-leaved or French sorrel, *Rumex scutatus*, which is smaller with a lighter flavor. The variegated cultivar 'Silver Shield' has silver-white patterning on its leaves. Red-veined sorrel or blood dock,

Rumex sanguineus var. *sanguineus*, has pointed green leaves with red veining. It can be more bitter than common sorrel and its leaves are best used young.

Grow in rich, moist but well-drained soil that is on the acidic side, in full sun or part-shade. Sorrel prefers cool conditions so will thrive in spring and fall but may bolt or go to seed quickly in the hot sun in summer.

Buy pot-grown plants and plant out any time from mid-spring up until late summer. Alternatively, sow seed in spring and summer. In early spring, sow under cover into plugs or pots of seed starting mix, covering thinly and watering in gently. Once seedlings are large enough to handle, pot on. Harden off and plant out in the garden once all risk of frost has passed. Alternatively, sow direct where they are to grow from late spring onward. Thin seedlings or space plants at least 12 in (30 cm) apart. You can also grow sorrel in containers.

Keep well watered, as sorrel will quickly bolt when dry. The leaves may also turn more bitter in hot weather. Prevent flowering by cutting off stems as they appear, and pinch out growing tips to encourage fresh, leafy growth.

In winter, the top growth will die back and can be removed. Mulch in winter or spring to restore nutrients. Watch out for damage from slugs.

PROPAGATE Sorrel will spread and needs to be divided every few years to stay productive. Dig up and split in spring or fall.

Red-veined sorrel is often grown as an ornamental, as well as edible, plant.

USES

Sorrel is used to add a grassy, lemony flavor. Young leaves can be eaten raw, chopped up finely to use as an herb like parsley and mint, used sparingly as a leaf vegetable in salads, or cooked as you would spinach or chard. More mature foliage should always be cooked, and can be used to flavor sauces; soup; and egg, fish, and seafood dishes.

Fresh young sorrel is eaten as a salad leaf or chopped to use as an herb.

HARVEST

Leaves should be ready to harvest about a month after planting, and can be picked over a long period from late spring through to fall and even sometimes into winter. Harvest regularly to promote growth of fresh young leaves. Use fresh, or freeze.

RUE *RUTA GRAVEOLENS*

Rue is a tough Mediterranean evergreen that forms a small bush with lacelike, glaucous green leaves, and clusters of yellow flowers in summer. Hardy and drought-tolerant, it is loved by butterflies but repels most other creatures, and should be handled with care.

PLANT TYPE Evergreen shrub
HARDINESS Hardy
HEIGHT 24–36 in (60–90 cm)
SPREAD 24 in (60 cm)
SOIL Any well-drained soil
LIGHT ☼
WARNING! Wear gloves when handling, as rue can cause severe allergic reactions; do not ingest as large amounts are toxic, and avoid completely when pregnant

Don't cut stems when wet or in full sun as they emit more allergen-causing chemicals then, and always use gloves. Avoid planting rue alongside paths or anywhere people may accidentally brush against it, as contact with the foliage and sap can cause allergic reactions and skin blisters or burns.

'Variegata' is less hardy than the other types and may need extra protection in very cold weather.

PROPAGATE Take softwood cuttings of new growth in early summer, or semi-hardwood cuttings in fall. In warm climates, rue will self-sow, or you can collect to sow the following spring.

HARVEST

Pick leaves or sprigs, in shade, during the growing season, and place on a rack or hang upside down to dry somewhere warm, dark, and dry.

When rue is wet it releases more chemicals that can irritate the skin.

Traditionally grown as an herb, rue's leaves and flowers are also ornamental.

GROW AND MAINTAIN

Ruta graveolens, common rue, is also called herb-of-grace and has pretty, deeply divided leaves that are lobed, with round edges. 'Jackman's Blue' has blue-gray foliage, while 'Variegata' has creamy white markings on new growth. Rue will grow in most well-drained soils, even poor and stony, but it most likes moderately fertile, sandy or loam soil, disliking heavy or clay soils, and prefers a position in full sun.

Buy pot-grown plants, or sow seeds of the species and variegated types under cover in spring on the surface of trays or small pots of seed starting mix. Water lightly and place somewhere warm to germinate. Once seedlings are large enough to handle, prick out or pot on. Harden off plants after all risk of frost has passed, and plant out in their final positions at least 18 in (45 cm) apart. Trim back plants after flowering and in spring to keep a compact form.

USES

Dried leaves can be used in sachets as moth repellent and to keep insects away. It has a strong smell that discourages most animals in the garden, including cats and dogs, but not butterflies. Rue has been a staple of herbal medicine for centuries, but it is best not to ingest this bitter herb, especially raw, as it can be poisonous in large quantities.

SAGE *SALVIA*

Sage has large, oval, gray-green leaves with a soft, often wrinkled texture, which stay on the plant all year, and pale purple flowers in summer. The foliage has a pungent musky-mint flavor and aroma with a hint of camphor, and is used sparingly, usually cooked rather than raw, in the kitchen.

PLANT TYPE Evergreen subshrub, perennial
HARDINESS Hardy, half-hardy
HEIGHT 24–36 in (60–90 cm)
SPREAD Up to 3 ft (1 m)
SOIL Light, neutral, well-drained soil
LIGHT ☼
WARNING! Ingesting large amounts of sage leaves can cause digestive upsets

Common sage, *Salvia officinalis,* is the form most used in the kitchen.

Sage's purple flowers are decorative in borders as well as in the herb garden.

Grow *Salvia officinalis* in a sheltered spot in full sun in any well-drained soil, except wet or heavy clay or very acid soils. The cultivars can't be grown from seed, so should be bought as ready-grown plants, which you can plant out once all risk of frost has passed in spring. Place plants in the ground at the same depth that they were in the pot, and water in well. Space them at least 18 in (45 cm) apart.

Purple sage makes an attractive mound-forming foliage plant for dry conditions.

GROW AND MAINTAIN

Salvia is a genus that includes many ornamental perennials grown for their summer flowers, but the one most used as a culinary herb is common sage, *Salvia officinalis*. There is a variety of this, known simply as broad-leaved sage, which has larger leaves than the species type, and is thought to have the best flavor. Both are hardy and, being Mediterranean plants, relatively drought-tolerant, with soft, slightly fuzzy, thin, green leaves. 'Berggarten' is another good variety, both for its flavor and its blue-purple flowers.

Some cultivars have attractively colored or patterned foliage, including 'Purpurascens', with purple young leaves; 'Icterina', a variegated type with yellow and green leaves; and 'Tricolor', which has pink-purple and green leaves with cream margins. These sages don't have as strong a scent or flavor as the common type, and are often less hardy.

For something fun and fruity, you could try the subtropical *Salvia elegans* 'Scarlet Pineapple', a half-hardy perennial sage with deliciously pineapple-scented leaves and masses of striking, bright red, tubular flowers in late summer.

The variegated leaves of 'Tricolor' add a bright accent to herb plantings.

Sow common sage seeds into small pots or trays of seed starting mix in early spring. The chances of germination are increased with a heated propagator. Prick out and pot on seedlings once they are large enough to handle. Harden young plants off and plant out in their final position once all risk of frost has passed. You can also sow seed direct where the plants are to grow in late spring. Thin seedlings to 18 in (45 cm) apart.

Sages, especially half-hardy ones like pineapple sage, can also be grown in containers in potting mix with added compost and perlite for drainage. Feed pot-grown plants with general fertilizer in spring. Young plants need to be watered while they establish and during dry spells, but don't overwater.

Mulch plants to offer them some protection over winter, or in the first year, cover with horticultural fleece when frost is forecast, and also if you live in a colder climate and wish to keep picking leaves throughout winter.

Pineapple sage should be brought under cover somewhere frost-free over winter.

Pineapple sage has strongly aromatic foliage that smells and tastes of pineapple.

PROPAGATE Take softwood cuttings in early summer.

PRUNE Sage needs an annual prune in spring to keep plants compact and vigorous. Cut back dead stems to just above where fresh growth is showing. Sage will not resprout from old wood, so don't cut into it. After flowering, trim back the plant all over to keep a neat shape. Despite regular cutting back, plants do tend to get leggy or woody

Sage needs to be pruned in spring and cut back regularly after flowering to keep it from becoming leggy.

at the base after a few years, and at that point they are best replaced. Don't prune in the fall.

HARVEST

Leaves can be picked throughout the year, and used fresh, but young foliage has the best flavor. To dry, hang upside down somewhere warm, dry, and dark for a couple of weeks. You can also try freezing leaves in ice cubes.

USES

Sage is most commonly used in the kitchen to flavor stuffing and dumplings. It makes the perfect partner for pumpkin recipes, sweet potato soup, mushrooms, and sharp-tasting cheeses like feta and goat cheese. It features in Italian dishes such as risotto, gnocchi, and veal saltimbocca, as well as sage butter sauce. It pairs well with pork and chicken roasts, and is a staple ingredient in sausages. Leaves can be used to make tea, but it should be drunk sparingly, as excessive ingestion can cause irritation.

Dried sage can sometimes have a strong, musty-dusty flavor but still have a good scent, which can make it better suited to potpourri.

Sage butter makes a delicious sauce for pasta.

ROSEMARY *SALVIA ROSMARINUS*

This fragrant evergreen is grown for its dark green, needlelike leaves, which have pale undersides, and an intense aroma and flavor of woody pine with citrus and pepper notes. Small blue, or occasionally pink or white, flowers appear in spring, and sometimes again throughout the year.

PLANT TYPE Evergreen subshrub
HARDINESS Hardy
HEIGHT Up to 6½ ft (2 m)
SPREAD Up to 6 ft (1.8 m)
SOIL Light, well-drained soil
LIGHT ☼

GROW AND MAINTAIN

Rosemary was previously known as *Rosmarinus officinalis*, but the name has been changed to *Salvia rosmarinus*, as it is actually a type of sage. There are many different cultivars available with a variety of growth habits, from low, mat-forming, ground cover types to upright, bushy shrubs. 'Miss Jessopp's Upright' is one of the most well-known and largest cultivars. Tall and erect, it reaches up to 6½ ft (2 m) high and wide, and bears blue flowers all down its stems from early spring to summer. It works very well as edging or hedging when planted in a row.

Prostratus Group is the opposite in form to the upright rosemaries, with a low, spreading or trailing habit, and an eventual height of just 8–12 in (20–30 cm). It has pale blue blooms in early spring. 'Severn Sea' is another trailing type, with mauve-blue blooms.

Other recommended blue-flowered varieties include *Salvia rosmarinus* var. *angustissimus* 'Benenden Blue', to 32 in (80 cm) with fine, narrow foliage and

The species, *Salvia rosmarinus*, is upright in form, with pale blue flowers.

Prostratus Group is a mat-forming rosemary, good for ground cover.

'Tuscan Blue' has flowers of a strong blue, and rich green foliage.

deep blue flowers; 'Tuscan Blue', with shorter, broader foliage and mid-blue flowers, to 3 ft (1 m); and 'McConnell's Blue', which has pale lilac-blue flowers and curled-edge leaves, and reaches around 20 in (50 cm).

If you want white flowers, there is *S. rosmarinus* (Albiflora Group) 'Lady in White'. There are also pink-flowered types including 'Roseus' and 'Majorca Pink'. For the most interesting scent and flavor, try 'Green Ginger', which has spicy notes. For form, 'Foxtail' wins the prize with its bushy, branched, arching stems and silvery leaf backs.

Originating from the Mediterranean, rosemary is easy to care for and quite drought-tolerant. While it is hardy down to around 14°F (−10°C), it can, nevertheless, be damaged by hard frosts, so needs a sheltered situation, such as at the base of a warm, south-facing wall, in full sun. Grow in moist but very well-drained, preferably light or sandy soil; it will not thrive in very acid or heavy clay soils, nor in wet winter conditions. You can also grow rosemary in containers in potting mix with compost added, but you will need to repot plants every year or two.

It is possible to sow seed of the species type in spring, but the cultivars will not come true from seed—that is, they will not have the attractive attributes and characteristics of the parent plants—and plants will not be ready for harvesting for a year or so. As such, it is best to start growing rosemary from pot-grown plants, which you can source online or from a garden center. Plant out in spring after all risk of frost has passed. If you need to improve drainage, add sand or well-rotted compost to the planting hole. Space plants at least 24 in (60 cm) apart or more, depending on variety.

Water plants regularly in the first season, while they establish, and as necessary during dry spells. Water those in containers more often, and feed with general fertilizer after flowering. Mulch plants to offer some protection over winter and use

'Green Ginger' has a spicy, gingery taste and flowers very freely.

horticultural fleece if frost is forecast in very exposed areas. Rosemary beetle can be a problem, as they can strip the foliage off plants. Pick these shiny, multicolored insects off by hand.

PROPAGATE Take softwood cuttings in spring or semi-hardwood (semi-ripe) cuttings in summer.

PRUNE Continual harvesting of rosemary will keep it neat, but most plants will also require regular pruning to keep them vigorous and compact, otherwise the stems will become leggy and bare at the base. Even when pruned, plants for the kitchen will probably need to be replaced every five years as they become less productive. Prune annually, in spring. Trim the plant all over by up to a third, and cut back the oldest, thickest stems to just a few sets of leaves. Never cut all the way back into old wood, as the plant will not reshoot from here—stay within the last season's growth, which will have green shoots or leaves. The exception is Prostratus Group, which only needs to be pruned very occasionally.

HARVEST

Rosemary is evergreen and grows all year, so you can pick sprigs or snip off stems any time, though it will produce the most fresh and flavorful growth in spring and summer. It is best used fresh, but you can also dry rosemary by hanging small bunches upside down in a warm, dry, dark place for a couple of weeks. Strip leaves off stems and store in an airtight container.

Rosemary and garlic make a classic flavoring for roasted potatoes.

USES

Rosemary can be added before and during cooking and is fantastic for flavoring roasts, especially lamb, chicken, and pork, as well as potatoes. It is often used together with balsamic vinegar for trays of roasted Mediterranean vegetables such as eggplant and squashes. Sprinkle cut leaves on to a potato and cheese pizza, or use whole sprigs in gravy, stews, and soups, and as a basting brush or as skewers for barbecues. Rosemary can be used to flavor vinegars and oils, or added in baking, for instance in focaccia and breadsticks.

'Roseus' is an upright rosemary with pastel pink flowers.

ELDER _SAMBUCUS NIGRA_

Elder is a large, bushy shrub or small tree with pretty, divided leaves that can be green, black, yellow, or variegated, and big, umbrella-shaped sprays of fragrant flowers in early summer. They are followed by small, usually black, sour berries in late summer to fall.

PLANT TYPE Deciduous shrub
HARDINESS Hardy
HEIGHT Up to 20 ft (6 m)
SPREAD Up to 12 ft (4 m)
SOIL Moist, well-drained soil
LIGHT ☼ ☼ ☀
WARNING! Don't ingest raw elderberries

Elder's huge flower heads add ornament and scent in the garden.

GROW AND MAINTAIN

Sambucus nigra, common elder, is also known as elderberry and European elder, and has flowers and berries that are edible when cooked. It should not be confused with American elder, _Sambucus canadensis_, all parts of which are poisonous. Common elder is a garden escapee, found growing wild in hedgerows and roadsides, among other places. It can be invasive if grown in the garden, so it may be preferable to forage for it elsewhere, or else plant one of the many well-behaved cultivars.

Cut-leaved elder, _S. nigra_ f. _laciniata_, is a good candidate with finely dissected, feathery leaves; creamy-white blooms; and dark purple berries. The cultivar 'Aurea', known as golden elder, has yellow leaves, and there are several dark-leaved types, including _S. nigra_ f. _porphyrophylla_ 'Black Lace' (syn. 'Eva'), which has divided, lacy, deep-purple foliage and pink flowers, and 'Black Beauty', with red-black leaves and dark pink blooms.

Elder prefers a sheltered, sunny position in moist but well-drained soil, but will tolerate a range of conditions, including heavy clay, chalky or poor soil, and anything from full sun to full shade.

Buy a pot-grown young specimen and plant in the fall. Water in well and keep watered while it establishes. Aside from this it needs little attention. Mulch each fall with organic matter.

PROPAGATE Take semi-hardwood cuttings in summer or fall.

PRUNE After about three years, shrubs should be established and can be pruned in spring. Remove dead and damaged growth, and cut out a few of the oldest stems. Elder can be cut back very hard to keep it to size or renovate an old plant, but you won't get flowers or fruit for one year afterward.

HARVEST

Depending on the weather, elder flowers appear in late spring to early summer. Pick in the morning on a dry, sunny day just as the buds have opened, cutting off the flowers with as little stalk as possible. Use immediately. Pick the berries from late summer on. If foraging from hedgerow plants, harvest away from roads, because of exhaust fumes, and pick higher up the plant to avoid contamination from animals.

Pick whole elderberry stalks but pop berries off the stalk when using.

USES

Elder flowers are used to make elderflower cordial and champagne, to flavor alcoholic drinks, and to make sugar syrup that can be used to flavor desserts. The flowers can also be battered and fried to eat as a sweet and tasty snack, dusted with powdered sugar. Elder berries are used to make wine, cordial, jam, and other preserves, and are baked in crumbles and pies. They must be cooked before eating, as they may cause digestive upsets when raw.

SALAD BURNET _SANGUISORBA MINOR_

This native herb is grown for its gray-green, tooth-edged foliage, which smells and tastes of cucumber. It also has rounded, knobbly flower heads, like crimson-red thimbles, from late spring to late summer. It is evergreen, and offers a pleasant sight, scent, and flavor all year.

PLANT TYPE Evergreen perennial
HARDINESS Hardy
HEIGHT Up to 18 in (45 cm)
SPREAD Up to 12 in (30 cm)
SOIL Any non-acidic, well-drained soil
LIGHT ☼ ☼

The **attractive foliage** of salad burnet can be picked throughout the year.

GROW AND MAINTAIN

Salad burnet, _Sanguisorba minor_, goes by a few different names, including garden burnet and pimpernelle. It is also known by its synonym _Poterium sanguisorba_. It forms a soft, neat mound of green all year and, as it is tough and hardy, it is easy to grow and care for.

It prefers a sheltered, sunny position in any well-drained soil but prefers a fertile, non-acidic, alkaline, or neutral soil.

Buy pot-grown plants or sow seed in spring. Start off indoors in trays or pots of seed starting mix, and plant out when all risk of frost has passed. Alternatively, direct sow outdoors onto prepared soil in late spring, in the spot where they are to grow. Space or thin plants to 12 in (30 cm) apart. Water in well and keep watered while they establish. They are drought-tolerant once settled in, but will produce lush growth if kept moist.

You can also grow salad burnet in containers. Keep well watered and feed with liquid fertilizer in spring.

Salad burnet has pretty little crimson flowers with long yellow stamens.

USES

The leaves can be used fresh throughout the year—just take the leaflets off the stalk and chop them up. As the name suggests, salad burnet is used in salads, and also to add flavor as a garnish for drinks like gin and tonic, or in place of mint or borage in summer dishes. Whip it into butter to make a tasty baste or topping for fish.

Salad burnet is fairly trouble-free, without any real problem pests or diseases or, aside from care in containers, any specific growing needs.

PROPAGATE Divide plants in the fall, or allow to flower and collect seed to store and sow in spring.

PRUNE For the best young leaves, don't allow it to flower but keep harvesting or cutting it back regularly to encourage fresh growth.

HARVEST

Leaves can be harvested around two months from sowing, and can be picked in moderation all year. Because of this, they are particularly welcome as ingredients for a winter salad. The young leaves have the best flavor and texture, so harvest little and often to keep plants productive.

COTTON LAVENDER *SANTOLINA*

PLANT TYPE Evergreen shrub
HARDINESS Hardy
HEIGHT 20–30 in (50–75 cm)
SPREAD Up to 3 ft (1 m)
SOIL Light, well-drained soil
LIGHT ☀

Cotton lavender is loved for its pretty year-round form and color. It has compact domes of silver-green leaves, which are thin, divided, and tooth-edged, and release a pleasant aroma when touched or brushed against. It also produces sulfur-yellow, button-like blooms from mid- to late summer.

A neat, silvery dome of cotton lavender adds structure in the garden.

'Lemon Queen' produces masses of pretty, creamy yellow flowers.

GROW AND MAINTAIN

Santolina chamaecyparissus is the main species known as cotton lavender, and has gray-green to silver foliage and bright yellow pinhead blooms. The cultivar 'Lemon Queen' has the same silvery leaf color but paler yellow to cream flowers. Other recommended cotton lavenders include *S. pinnata* subsp. *neapolitana* 'Edward Bowles', which has creamy-white flowers; *S. rosmarinifolia* 'Lemon Fizz', which has golden-yellow to green, finely dissected foliage; and *S. rosmarinifolia* subsp. *rosmarinifolia* 'Primrose Gem', with bright green leaves and pale yellow blooms.

Cotton lavender thrives in full sun, and although fairly hardy, it should be placed in a sheltered position, as it can be damaged in temperatures below around 14°F (−10°C) and so needs extra protection such as horticultural fleece in very cold weather. It will happily tolerate poor or stony soils, but will grow lax in rich soil and may rot off in heavy, wet soils. It will grow best in a light or sandy well-drained soil.

It is not easy to grow from seed, so buy pot-grown plants to start, and plant out in spring after all risk of frost has passed, or in the fall. You can also plant in summer if you are able to monitor the plant's water needs while it establishes. Space plants at least 24 in (60 cm) apart, or 12–16 in (30–40 cm) for a row or hedge.

Cotton lavender is quite drought-tolerant, once established, but don't let it dry out completely while it settles in.

Many gardeners grow the plant only for its foliage and do not like the blooms, so they pinch them out or snip them off as they appear.

PROPAGATE Take softwood cuttings before plants flower, in spring or early summer, or semi-hardwood cuttings in summer or fall.

PRUNE It's important to trim the whole plant back after flowering to maintain a compact form, or it may become leggy and the base and center may become bare. Also prune in early spring, cutting back to within about 1 in (3 cm) of where last season's growth begins, above where it meets the old growth.

HARVEST

Pick leaves before the plant flowers. To dry, hang bunches upside down somewhere dark, warm, and dry for about two weeks.

USES

In the home, the dried leaves can be used in potpourri, and are particularly effective as a moth repellent. Add dried leaves to cloth sachets and place in your drawers and wardrobe. In the garden, cotton lavender gives year-round structure and scent, so works well as edging or clipped mounds.

SAVORY *SATUREJA*

This small, aromatic, bushy herb looks a lot like thyme, with stems covered in many tiny, linear green leaves, and white or pinky-mauve blooms in summer. It tastes a little like thyme as well, but with a more peppery flavor, and the plant as a whole has a spicy sweet scent.

PLANT TYPE Semi-evergreen subshrub, annual
HARDINESS Hardy, half-hardy
HEIGHT Up to 12 in (30 cm)
SPREAD Up to 12 in (30 cm)
SOIL Light, well-drained soil
LIGHT ☼

GROW AND MAINTAIN

There are two main types of culinary savory. Summer savory, *Satureja hortensis*, is a half-hardy annual plant with bright green leaves and white or pale purple blooms. It has to be sown fresh each season, and likes a sheltered position. It is also called bean herb.

Winter savory, *Satureja montana*, is a semi-evergreen woody perennial or subshrub, which has dark green leaves that, as the name suggests, are usually retained throughout winter, though it may lose some leaves and the foliage can start to look sparse. It also has pink or white flowers, and will live in the garden for a number of years from first sowing or planting.

Grow both types in poor to moderately fertile, light, well-drained, neutral to alkaline soil, in full sun. Savory can also be grown in containers, if your soil is too heavy, acidic, or wet.

Buy pot-grown plants in spring, or start seeds off under cover in early spring. Sow onto the surface of trays of moist seed starting mix. Prick out and pot on once seedlings are large enough to handle. Harden off and plant out in the garden only once all risk of frost has passed. Space plants 6–12 in (15–30 cm) apart. Water in well. Pinch back tips as the plants grow to promote bushy, compact growth.

At the end of the season, summer savory can be lifted and discarded on the compost heap. Container-grown

USES

Savory is often used in making salami and stuffing, and is a main ingredient in *herbes de Provence* mix. Add sprigs of leaves when roasting vegetables and meat; they also go well with beans. Savory can be used as a salt replacement, and is a popular choice for flavored vinegars and oils. Both types should be used sparingly at first as they are strong and spicy to taste, though summer savory has a lighter, less pungent flavor.

winter savory and plants in exposed gardens will benefit from extra protection such as horticultural fleece during very cold weather.

PROPAGATE Take softwood cuttings of winter savory in late spring or early summer, before flowering.

PRUNE Trim back winter savory in spring, removing old and dead growth. Keep both types trimmed or harvest continually to keep a nice compact and productive form.

HARVEST

Pick leaves of summer savory regularly throughout the growing season and stop it from flowering to keep the best flavor. Winter savory can be picked from spring through to early winter.

Winter savory should be trimmed regularly to keep a good shape.

MILK THISTLE *SILYBUM MARIANUM*

The most striking feature of milk thistle is its large, spiky, green foliage with white marbled patterning. It also produces tall stems topped with artichoke-like flower heads with purple blooms and spiny bracts. It is loved by bees, butterflies, and birds.

PLANT TYPE Deciduous biennial
HARDINESS Hardy
HEIGHT Up to 5 ft (1.5 m)
SPREAD Up to 3 ft (1 m)
SOIL Light, well-drained soil
LIGHT ☀ ◑
WARNING! Toxic to livestock—don't plant near boundaries in rural locations—and wear gloves when handling

The attractive flowers of milk thistle form in the summer of its second year.

GROW AND MAINTAIN

Silybum marianum is an upright biennial, also known as blessed Mary's thistle. It produces a rosette of leaves in its first year, and then leaves and flowers in its second season. It can tolerate a range of conditions, which makes it very easy to grow—so easy that it is seen as invasive in some regions, such as parts of North America and Australia.

Milk thistle prefers a light, loamy or sandy, well-drained soil that is neutral to alkaline, but will grow in most soils as long as it doesn't experience very wet, cold winters. It likes full sun best but will manage light or part shade, too.

Sow seeds outdoors, where they are to grow, in late spring or early summer, placing about ½ in (1 cm) deep and covering over. Water in well. Thin out to about 36 in (90 cm) apart.

You can also grow milk thistle in containers under cover—this may be the best option in places where the plant is considered invasive, as this will restrict the dispersal of the seed. If growing indoors, be aware that they will develop into tall and spiky plants. Sow seed in trays of seed starting mix. Once they are large enough to handle, prick out seedlings and pot on.

Milk thistle is a fairly drought-resistant plant, but keep it well-watered while it establishes and in very dry periods. If you want to grow it for the beautiful foliage, remove the flower stalks as they appear.

Top growth can be removed once the plant has died back for winter, but be careful when handling as many parts of the plant are spiky. It will return the following spring and flower that summer before dying back completely.

PROPAGATE Milk thistle seeds are viable for up to a decade, and are spread far and wide by the wind, so once you grow it, you will probably find many plants of it popping up around the garden without any intervention needed from you. To control this, collect whole flower heads just as they start to dry out and white fluffy tufts begin to appear. Separate out the seed and sow the following season.

HARVEST

Harvest seed as explained above, but cut the flowers off with the shortest amount of stem possible. Dry in a paper bag for up to two weeks and then scrunch up to release the seed. Separate out seed from the flower head and white fluff. Store in an airtight container.

USES

Many parts of the milk thistle are edible but it is grown mostly for its seeds. They are used, sometimes with the dried leaves, to make a popular herbal tea, and can also be eaten like flax seeds by adding to smoothies, salads, cereal, and as an ingredient in baked cakes or bread.

To make milk thistle tea, steep seeds in hot water and then strain.

STEVIA *STEVIA REBAUDIANA*

Stevia is a subtropical plant that originates from South America, where it has been used as a natural sweetener for centuries. The leaves are green and ovate with gently notched edges, and have a hint of licorice in flavor. White flowers appear in late summer.

PLANT TYPE Evergreen perennial
HARDINESS Tender
HEIGHT Up to 24 in (60 cm)
SPREAD Up to 18 in (45 cm)
SOIL Light, moist but well-drained soil
LIGHT ☀ ☀

Stevia leaves are used as a powerful natural sweetener.

The flowers are pretty, but for best leaf flavor remove buds as they form.

GROW AND MAINTAIN

Stevia rebaudiana is an upright bushy perennial also known as caa-ehe, sweet leaf, or candyleaf. It is tender—it won't survive winter outside in cold climates—and so is often grown as an annual, or in a container that can be brought inside in winter or kept indoors all year.

If growing outdoors as an annual, in the ground or in a container, choose a warm, bright, sheltered south- or west-facing spot. Stevia prefers a light or sandy, well-drained, neutral to slightly acid soil. It needs to stay moist during the summer, but drier in winter. If growing indoors, choose a bright situation, like a windowsill, out of drafts and away from heat sources such as vents.

You can buy and sow seeds indoors in spring, and place in a heated propagator to germinate, but this can be a slow and erratic process, so it is best to start with pot-grown plants or plugs. Plant in the ground, or in pots of enriched potting mix, outside after all risk of frost has passed. Space at least 8 in (20 cm) apart. Water in well, and keep soil moist while it establishes.

Bring pots indoors in the fall before the first frost or, if growing as an annual, lift and discard plants on the compost heap. In winter, water indoor plants only very occasionally when the soil is dry. In spring, repot into a larger container and begin watering again.

PROPAGATE Take cuttings of fresh shoots that have not formed flower heads in early summer.

PRUNE If growing indoors over winter, cut back the top growth to around 6 in (15 cm) when you bring it under cover in the fall.

USES

Stevia leaves are used, dried or fresh, to make a sweet water, extract, or syrup. They are also widely used to add a sweet, slightly earthy taste when cooking or when brewing tea. Stevia has been used for hundreds of years in South America for its sweet flavor and, because it contains virtually no calories, it is now manufactured into a sugar-replacement sweetener, which is used all over the world. It is sold in dried or processed form as a health supplement in most regions. However, owing to a lack of internationally recognized research on the effects of ingesting unprocessed fresh or dried leaves, their use as a food ingredient is not recommended in some countries.

HARVEST

Leaves can be harvested as needed from about 6–8 weeks from planting. The flavor is only good before the plant blooms, so keep pinching out tips, harvesting leaves, and snipping off flower stems and buds as they form, to prevent flowering. Dry bunches by hanging upside down for about two weeks, or dry the leaves individually on a rack, somewhere warm but dry and dark; alternatively, use a dehydrator. Store in an airtight container.

COMFREY *SYMPHYTUM*

A relative of borage, comfrey is often seen growing wild in damp places. It has big, hairy green leaves and clusters of small, bell-shaped blooms in pink, purple, or cream, which are attractive to bees. It is prized by gardeners as a source of nutrition for other plants.

PLANT TYPE Deciduous perennial
HARDINESS Hardy
HEIGHT Up to 4 ft (1.2 m)
SPREAD 3 ft (1 m) or more
SOIL Any well-drained soil
LIGHT ☼ ◐
WARNING! Ingestion may cause severe discomfort; wear gloves when handling and wash hands afterward

'Variegatum' is the most attractive-looking comfrey cultivar.

GROW AND MAINTAIN

Symphytum officinale, common comfrey, also called bruisewort and knitbone, is tough, hardy, and spreading. It forms clumps of upright stems to about 3 ft (1 m), lined with elliptic-shaped foliage and topped with bunches of pendent flowers in late spring or early summer.

Symphytum × uplandicum, Russian comfrey, is taller, to around 4 ft (1.2 m), with lance-shaped green leaves and pink or purple flowers. The cultivar 'Bocking 14' is the best choice for gardeners, because it is sterile and therefore won't spread through self-seeding, and is high in nutrients. 'Variegatum' has green and cream-edged leaves and pale purple blooms. It is not as invasive as the species but where to grow it still needs to be considered.

Comfrey develops very long roots and will thrive in most situations. Grow in moist but well-drained soil in full sun or part shade. All types except 'Bocking 14' will spread indefinitely, so site with care: ideally plant it in a small bed on its own to keep it contained.

Seed germination is erratic and slow, so it is best to buy plants or bare-root crowns (dormant plants sold without soil) to start. Plant in spring, growing crowns on in a pot under cover, and planting out once leaves appear and all risk of frost has passed. Alternatively, plant out directly in the fall. Place crowns around 6 in (15 cm) deep—a little less if the soil is heavy. Pot-grown plants can be planted out at the same level they were at in the pot. Space plants 20–30 in (50–75 cm) apart.

Water in well, and keep the plants well-watered until they are established. Cut back after flowering, and remove dead foliage when the plant dies back in the fall.

PROPAGATE The easiest way to propagate is division or root cuttings in spring.

HARVEST

Once plants are established, you can cut leaves down several times a year, from spring to fall. Use shears and wear gloves, as the hairs on the leaves and stems are prickly.

USES

Comfrey is most valuable for the extraordinarily rich amount of nutrients found in its leaves. They are used as an accelerator on the compost heap, or chopped up as a mulch around edible plants, and can be used to make "comfrey tea," a healthy liquid fertilizer. Chop up the leaves and pack them, with a little water, into a watertight container with a lid; in larger containers, use a brick to weigh the leaves down. After about four weeks, the leaves will have rotted down, leaving an extremely stinky brown liquid in the bottom of the container. Strain it into a bottle or plastic milk carton. To use, dilute this concentrate with water, in a 1:10 ratio, and feed it to your garden plants.

Weighing down comfrey leaves in a container helps them rot.

FEVERFEW
TANACETUM PARTHENIUM

Feverfew is a cheery, bushy herb with fragrant green or yellow leaves divided in lacy patterns, and small, perky, daisylike flowers with yellow centers and white petals. It is so called as it was once believed to cure fevers. This hardy perennial is very attractive to bees.

PLANT TYPE Semi-evergreen or deciduous perennial
HARDINESS Hardy
HEIGHT Up to 24 in (60 cm)
SPREAD Up to 20 in (50 cm)
SOIL Light, well-drained soil
LIGHT ☼
WARNING! Ingesting the leaves may irritate the inside of the mouth

Pretty flowers and bright, lacy leaves make feverfew a decorative garden plant.

GROW AND MAINTAIN

Tanacetum is a genus containing a number of herbs, including feverfew, *T. parthenium*. Previously known as *Chrysanthemum parthenium*, feverfew is tall and bushy with green leaves and clusters of long-lasting flowers in summer. The smaller cultivar 'Aureum', golden feverfew, has yellow leaves. There is a variety which is called simply *T. parthenium* double white-flowered, often sold as 'Flore Pleno', with small white double blooms. Another good form is called 'White Bonnet', which has showy, spherical, pompom-like double flowers. Other rare cultivars worth seeking out include 'Selma Star', 'Malmesbury', and 'Snowball'.

Feverfew prefers a light, fertile, well-drained soil in full sun, and hates heavy clay or wet soils. Buy pot-grown plants or sow seed directly where they are to grow in spring. You can also start plants off under cover in early spring or fall by sowing into pots of seed starting mix, lightly covering, and watering in. Prick out and pot on once seedlings are large enough to handle. Harden off once all risk of frost has passed, before planting out in their final position. Space at least 12 in (30 cm) apart.

Feverfew is quite drought-tolerant once it is settled, but keep plants well-watered while they establish. Deadhead regularly to stop them from self-sowing around, and cut back plants after flowering to encourage a fresh flush of growth. Watch out for damage from aphids. In mild climates and winters, these plants can keep some of their leaves over winter. Remove any dead foliage or stems in spring.

Although it is perennial, feverfew can be short-lived, so don't be surprised if a plant only lasts for a few years. Fortunately, it is easy to propagate.

PROPAGATE Feverfew will self-seed happily if allowed, providing lots of seedlings. You can also divide plants in spring or fall, or take cuttings of nonflowering shoots in summer.

HARVEST

Harvest leaves from early summer to early fall, and flowers as they open. To dry, hang upside down somewhere dark, warm, and dry for up to 10 days.

USES

All *Tanacetum* species have proven insect-repellent powers. Dried leaves of feverfew can be placed in sachets in wardrobes and chests of drawers to keep out moths. The dried flowers make a nice addition to potpourri. It is claimed the fresh leaves help ease migraine headaches; they are usually recommended to be eaten between slices of bread as they are very bitter and can irritate the inside of the mouth.

DANDELION *TARAXACUM*

Widely considered a garden weed, dandelion is a tough and hardy herb once grown as a leaf crop. It produces a rosette of lance-shaped serrated green leaves, with a bitter flavor, and brilliant yellow flowers from spring to fall, followed by white puffball seed heads.

PLANT TYPE Semi-evergreen or deciduous perennial
HARDINESS Hardy
HEIGHT 6–24 in (15–60 cm)
SPREAD Up to 12 in (30 cm)
SOIL Any soil
LIGHT ☼ ☼

Dandelion's fluffy seed heads spread seeds far and wide on the wind.

GROW AND MAINTAIN

Although wild dandelion, *Taraxacum officinale*, is now thought of as a difficult-to-eradicate weed, it was originally cultivated as a food plant, and there are several "gourmet" cultivars available. Two of the most popular are French dandelion, *T. officinale* 'Vert de Montmagny', a heritage type with a mild flavor and broad leaves, and the variety sold as Improved Thick-Leaved, which grows up to 24 in (60 cm) tall; is slow to bolt; and has large, fleshy leaves. Other interesting dandelions include the white-flowered *T. albidum*, and *T. pseudoroseum*, which has pink flowers with yellow centers.

Dandelions are not fussy and will grow almost anywhere. However, they will be at their tastiest and least bitter when grown in fertile, loamy, deep, and moist but well-drained soil in full sun or part shade. They are perennial, but some gardeners advise growing as annuals for the best flavor.

Sow seeds in spring or fall. Start them off under cover in early spring, on the surface of moist seed starting mix in tall root trainer plugs or deep pots. Place somewhere bright, and keep the soil moist to encourage germination. Once the seedlings are large enough to handle, and all risk of frost has passed, plant them out where they are to grow. Space plants at least 6 in (15 cm) apart, or more for Improved Thick-Leaved. Dandelions are not the ideal candidates for pots because of their long taproots, but you can grow them in deep containers.

These plants are extremely low-maintenance and untroubled by pests and diseases but, for the best leaves, keep well watered. All dandelion varieties will self-sow widely, so remove the flower stalks to prevent this.

PROPAGATE The best way to propagate is to take root cuttings in spring or fall—simply dig up a plant, cut up the root, and plant the pieces.

HARVEST

For the best-tasting leaves and roots, remove flower heads as they form. Pick young, fresh leaves regularly, snipping them off at the base. To blanch leaves for the most tender growth, hill up the base of the plant or tie the leaves up and cover with something that will block out the light, such as an upside-down pot, for a few weeks. Harvest roots in the fall and dry before using. If growing for flowers, harvest them as they open, and discard the stalks.

Both the leaves and the root of the dandelion are tasty food ingredients.

USES

All parts of dandelions, apart from the flower stems, are edible. The leaves are used young and fresh in salads, and can be cooked like you would spinach. The roots can be roasted and ground up to make a coffee-like drink, or dandelion and burdock root beer. The flowers are often used to make dandelion wine.

FENUGREEK *TRIGONELLA FOENUM-GRAECUM*

Fenugreek, an exotic legume, produces hollow, hairy, branching stems covered with three-part, ovate green foliage and topped with pale creamy-yellow to white, sweet-scented blooms from midsummer. They are followed by bean-like yellow pods filled with small brown-yellow seeds.

PLANT TYPE Annual
HARDINESS Half-hardy
HEIGHT Up to 24 in (60 m)
SPREAD 6 in (15 cm)
SOIL Any well-drained soil
LIGHT ☼

Fenugreek, like other legumes, has pea plant–like leaves and flowers.

Square-shaped seeds are produced in bean-like pods.

GROW AND MAINTAIN

Also called Greek clover or methi, fenugreek originates from the warm climates of southeastern Europe, west Asia, and India. It is an easy-to-grow plant that is versatile in the garden and kitchen. The flowers smell like maple syrup, and the leaves and seeds have a curry-like, slightly bitter, spicy flavor.

Grow in any fertile, well-drained soil in full sun. It needs a long, bright, warm season of growing to set seed in cooler climates, so in these regions, it is best to sow under cover in spring. Fenugreek hates it when its roots are disturbed, so sow seed into biodegradable plug modules or pots that you can plant out later completely, without transplanting.

Once all risk of frost has passed, harden off seedlings and then plant out in their final position. In warmer climates, where late frosts are not an issue, you can start off earlier outdoors by sowing seeds directly where the plants are to grow in mid spring. Space or thin out seedlings to at least 4 in (10 cm) apart. Fenugreek can also be grown in containers.

Water in well and keep well-watered. Pinch out tips regularly to encourage compact, bushy growth. Once the foliage has died back and any seeds have been harvested, you can lift and discard the plants on the compost heap.

PROPAGATE Collect pods and extract seed from them in late summer or fall, before storing in an airtight container to sow the following season.

HARVEST

Harvest leaves before the plant flowers, picking as required from the top of the plant, leaving some growth at the base of the foliage. Plants will flower and then set seed toward the end of the season. Harvest seed pods once leaves begin to turn yellow. Snap them off the stems and peel the pods open to get to the seed.

USES

Fenugreek seeds are widely used in Indian cuisine as well as throughout the Mediterranean, Middle East, and parts of north Africa. Roasted and used whole or ground, they are a vital ingredient in curries, pickles, and chutneys, and in spice mixes such as *garam masala*, *panch phoran* (Indian five-spice), or in dry rubs for meat. The fresh leaves are used to garnish dishes and added to salads. The seeds are also used for sprouts and microgreens. When using as a spice in home cooking, dry-roast the seeds first in a frying pan.

Fenugreek seeds can be used whole or ground.

THYME *THYMUS*

Thyme is grown for its very small, short, green or gray-green leaves that have a slightly woody, sweet floral aroma and an earthy flavor with subtle hints of mint and citrus. In spring and summer, most thymes produce pink, purple, or white flowers, which are a magnet for bees and other pollinators.

PLANT TYPE Evergreen subshrub
HARDINESS Hardy
HEIGHT Up to 12 in (30 cm)
SPREAD Up to 32 in (80 cm)
SOIL Light, well-drained soil
LIGHT ☼

GROW AND MAINTAIN

Common thyme, *Thymus vulgaris*, grows to around 12 in (30 cm) tall and wide, and has thin, dark-green leaves, and mauve flowers in summer. It is great in the kitchen and widely available. However, there are about 200 other types and varieties, with diverse leaf size and color, and different growth habits from low, mat-forming ground covers to mounding types and taller upright forms.

Lemon thyme is just as popular as common thyme. However, there are several lemon-scented cultivars, and uncertainty over whether the species *T. citriodorus* or *T. × citriodorus* is accepted as a type in its own right or not. As a result, lots of different plants are sold as lemon thyme. Some of the best ones for lemon flavor include *T.* 'Golden King', which has yellow and green variegated leaves, growing

'Golden King' has strongly lemon-scented leaves with bright yellow edges.

to 12 in (30 cm); 'Archers Gold' to 8 in (20 cm), with bright lime-yellow leaves; and *T. pulegioides* 'Aureus', to 8 in (20 cm), with golden-yellow leaves. *T.* 'Silver Queen' is also lemon-scented and has dark green leaves with cream-white margins, on red-hued stems.

For interesting gold or silver leaves and a pure thyme scent and flavor, try *T. pulegioides* 'Bertram Anderson', which creates a neat mound of yellow leaves and pink summer flowers, to 4 in (10 cm); or *T.* 'Silver Posie', with white variegated leaves and pale pink blooms to 12 in (30 cm).

Other cultivars worth seeking out for flavor include *T.* 'Fragrantissimus', orange-scented thyme, which has gray-green leaves, and pale pink

flowers, to 12 in (30 cm); and *Thymus herba-barona*, caraway thyme, which has spicy caraway and citrus flavored foliage. It reaches just 1¼–2 in (3–5 cm) high, forming a low spreading mat.

There are many very low-growing types like this, such as *T. serpyllum* 'Annie Hall', with green leaves and pretty pale-pink blooms; creeping red thyme, *T.* Coccineus Group, which has bright magenta-pink flowers and dark green leaves; and *T. serpyllum* 'Minor', a sweet little dwarf form with tiny green leaves. They work well in thyme walks and lawns, gravel plantings, and in cracks or joints in paving (see *p.25*). Another good choice for these situations is 'Bressingham', to 8 in (20 cm), with gray-green leaves and pink flowers.

The flowers of common thyme are pretty and pollinator-friendly.

Mound-forming thymes make a good, informal edging in beds and borders.

Grow in a sheltered spot in full sun, in very well-drained soil. Thyme doesn't mind poor, sandy, or stony soils, and is drought-tolerant once established, but will suffer in wet cold winters and heavy soils. Common thyme can be grown from seed but cultivars will only come true, or have the parent plant's features, from cuttings, so in almost all cases it is best to start growing thyme by buying a ready-grown plant.

If you do wish to sow seeds, start them off in early spring under cover in pots or trays of seed starting mix, water lightly, and place in a propagator to germinate. Once the seedlings are large enough to handle, prick them out into individual pots. Harden off and plant out in the garden when all risk of frost has passed.

Space plants at least 8 in (20 cm) apart, depending on how spreading the variety is. Water in well and then as necessary during their first season, allowing the soil to dry out between waterings, but only water occasionally or during very dry periods after they are well established.

You can also grow thyme in containers; it does best in potting mix with added compost and perlite. Water when the soil dries out during the growing season, and then only rarely in winter. Feed plants in pots with a general-purpose fertilizer in spring and summer.

PROPAGATE Take softwood cuttings in early spring, before flowering, or from new growth that appears after flowering in summer. Creeping, spreading thymes can often be divided in late spring.

PRUNE After flowering, trim back plants all over to encourage fresh growth and keep a neat form. Plants that are not pruned will quickly become woody and bare toward the base and center, and will need to be replaced.

HARVEST

As an evergreen, thyme can be picked all year, but the best time to harvest for flavor is in spring and early summer, before flowering. Use fresh, store in the fridge in a food storage bag for a few days, or leave out uncovered to dry.

'Bressingham' grows well in dry, stony ground and in paving cracks

'Silver Queen' has attractive variegated foliage and red stems.

USES

Thyme is a main component in herb mixes like *bouquet garni* and *herbes de Provence*. It is used to flavor stuffing, stews, and casseroles, roasts such as chicken and pork, and fish dishes. It works well with egg recipes; with mushrooms, onions, and potatoes; and for flavored oil and vinegar. Lemon thyme is a popular flavoring for cakes, desserts, and cocktails. Use whole sprigs or stripped leaves.

Strip thyme leaves from their stems by running your index finger and thumb down the stalk.

NASTURTIUM *TROPAEOLUM MAJUS*

Nasturtiums are one of the easiest flowers to grow, quickly producing an abundance of brightly colored edible summer blooms with long spurs in shades of red, orange, and yellow. The foliage is round and green, occasionally mottled, and the large seeds can be eaten, too.

PLANT TYPE Annual
HARDINESS Half-hardy
HEIGHT Up to 6 ft (1.8 m)
SPREAD Up to 30 in (75 cm)
SOIL Any well-drained soil
LIGHT ☼

Nasturtium flowers are beautiful as well as edible.

GROW AND MAINTAIN

Tropaeolum majus is an annual climber or trailing plant, also known as Indian cress. There are many cultivars, with a variety of flower colors and foliage effects, and some with a bushy habit.

You will often find seed mixes for sale with names such as "Trailing Mixed," with yellow, red, and orange flowers. One popular variety is Alaska Series, which has a bushy to semi-trailing habit, and variegated green and cream leaves. 'Empress of India' is another widely available type, with deep red flowers and dark green leaves. Tip Top Velvet also has red blooms, and 'Hermine Grashoff' has double red flowers. 'Salmon Gleam' is an unusual apricot-cream variety with red centers, while 'Salmon Baby' has brighter coral-pink blooms. The flowers of 'Milkmaid' are cream to white, while those of 'Banana Split' are bright yellow.

Grow in a sheltered spot in full sun, in any well-drained but preferably poor soil. Rich soil (or feeding nasturtiums) will result in lots of lush leafy growth but few flowers.

The simplest approach is to sow nasturtiums directly where they are to flower in late spring, or any time up to midsummer. Once the risk of frost has passed, sow two seeds to a hole about ½ in (2 cm) deep, and water in well. You can also sow under cover in early to mid-spring, placing seeds in plugs or small pots of seed starting mix and covering lightly. Keep moist and plant seedlings out after all risk of frost.

Thin or space plants out to at least 12 in (30 cm) apart. To have continuous harvests right through to fall, sow successionally, a few every week.

If growing in pots, window boxes, or hanging baskets, add plenty of perlite to the growing mix to ensure good drainage. Provide supports such as bamboo tripods, or a trellis for climbing

Nasturtiums planted next to beans help keep aphids away from the crop.

varieties, or simply allow them to romp through other plants and along the ground as trailers.

Nasturtiums are fast-growing and low-maintenance, thriving on neglect. Water occasionally during dry periods and those in pots regularly. Deadhead flowers to encourage further blooms. Watch out for aphids and caterpillars.

PROPAGATE Allow plants to set seed after flowering and collect when ripe. Store in an airtight container to sow the following spring. Nasturtiums will also self-seed around if permitted.

HARVEST

Pick leaves young for the best flavor—they get hot to bitter the larger and more mature they are. Flowers will appear about 2–3 months after sowing, from summer to fall. Seed can be harvested for the kitchen when ripe and mature, but still green.

USES

Nasturtium leaves and flowers add a peppery taste to salads, and the flowers also make a tasty garnish for cakes and cocktails. The seeds can be pickled in vinegar and used as a replacement for capers. In the garden, nasturtiums are used as a companion plant to attract aphids away from vegetable plants.

NETTLE *URTICA DIOICA*

Nettles have tough, upright stems lined with dark green, ovate, tooth-edged leaves. They are covered in small, bristly hairs that cause a deeply unpleasant stinging sensation when touched. Nettles also produce green-yellow to brown, catkin-like flowers in late spring, which persist into early fall.

PLANT TYPE Deciduous perennial
HARDINESS Hardy
HEIGHT Up to 5 ft (1.5 m)
SPREAD Up to 13 ft (4 m) or more
SOIL Any well-drained soil
LIGHT ☼ ☼ ☼
WARNING! Contact will cause painful skin irritation, so wear gloves and protective gear

GROW AND MAINTAIN

Stinging nettle, *Urtica dioica*, is usually seen as an invasive, unwanted weed, but it is also a highly nutritious herb, packed with vitamin C and iron. You are not likely to find it for sale, but it is abundantly available on verges, woodland, pasture edges, hedgerows, and, of course, most gardens, too, so it is simple to source. You can easily find an unwanted patch of nettles and, wearing gloves, dig it up and transplant it to your chosen site in the garden.

Nettles love fertile soil that is moist but well-drained, and a sunny position, but will tolerate a range of conditions. They will grow in part or full shade, in any aspect, and are very hardy. Their many stinging prickly hairs are found on the undersides of the serrated, arrow-shaped leaves and on the stems. The sting hurts on contact, and continues with painful pins-and-needles feelings for some time, so nettles need to be handled, and sited, carefully. Grow them away from where anyone might accidentally brush past and especially where children play.

Nettles are highly invasive, so you may want to keep them to a restricted area, such as a separate bed or a container. Watch out for and remove the rooting stems that creep along the surface of the soil, and don't let nettles flower and seed, or they will take over. However, if you have space to grow a large patch of nettles in the sun, this is really beneficial for wildlife such as butterflies, ladybugs, and birds.

The fresh green leaves of nettles are tasty and lose their sting when cooked.

Be sure to wear gloves when harvesting nettle leaves.

USES

Nettles are a popular plant to use for boiled or steamed spring greens, nettle tea, and nettle soup. The sting is removed by hot water or steam. They can be used as a replacement in any recipe that calls for spinach, and can be treated in the same way. They are often used in dishes like risotto, gnocchi, quiche, pesto, and rarebit. Nettles have been used historically to make dyes, and for string and textiles. They can also be used to make a plant feed, in the same way as for comfrey (see p.128)

PROPAGATE Take root cuttings or let nettles spread via their roots and rooting stems.

HARVEST

Nettles are best harvested when the leaves are young and tender, and before they flower, particularly in spring. You can also trim or cut back nettles in summer to promote fresh young growth. The best leaves to eat are the freshest 4–6 at the top of each plant or the bright green tips of side shoots. When collecting leaves, wear thick gardening or dishwashing gloves, a long-sleeved top, and long pants, to protect your skin. Wear gloves or use tongs to prepare the leaves for cooking, and wash thoroughly before using.

VALERIAN *VALERIANA OFFICINALIS*

Loved by pollinators, valerian is a tall, upright, branching perennial with divided, tooth-edged, dark green leaves. In late spring and summer, it produces domed clusters of tiny white to pale pink flowers. The blooms have a sweet scent but the roots emit a stinky odor when disturbed.

PLANT TYPE Deciduous perennial
HARDINESS Hardy
HEIGHT Up to 5 ft (1.5 m)
SPREAD Up to 36 in (90 cm)
SOIL Any moist but well-drained soil
LIGHT ☀ ◐

Valerian flowers have a lovely scent and are produced all summer long.

GROW AND MAINTAIN

Valeriana officinalis, also known as garden heliotrope, is a native British plant often thought of as wild, as it can often be found growing in damp conditions outside the garden, such as in ditches or by streams. It is a popular choice for wildlife and cottage gardens because of its pretty blooms, which attract beneficial insects from bees and butterflies to lacewings and hoverflies. It will come back every year and develop into a large clump over time.

Valerian will tolerate a wide range of conditions including part shade and any well-drained soil, but for best results, grow in a moist but well-drained soil, in full sun. They are hungry plants, and will benefit from rich soil with organic matter incorporated into the planting hole, or regular feeding through the season.

The spiky, finely divided foliage of valerian is also attractive in the garden.

Although valerian can be grown from seed, germination is often poor and erratic. It is probably easiest to buy seedlings, plugs, or young plants, and plant them in mid- to late spring, after all risk of frost has passed, or in the fall. To try raising from seed, sow indoors in early spring onto the surface of plugs or small pots of seed starting mix. Place somewhere bright and keep moist. Harden off seedlings once all risk of frost has passed and plant out in their final position. You can also sow directly where they are to grow once all risk of frost has passed, pressing the seed into the surface of the soil. Thin out seedlings or space plants to at least 24 in (60 cm) apart.

Keep well watered while plants establish. Deadhead flowers before they set seed to stop them from self-sowing. Cut back to the ground in the fall.

PROPAGATE Valerian is a vigorous self-seeder and seedlings that appear beneath the parent plant can be transplanted to other locations. It also spreads underground and can be dug up and divided in spring or fall.

HARVEST

Flower stems and leaves can be cut or picked as desired in summer. For the root, choose plants two or more years old. Dig up a whole root. Wash it, take off the skinny, fibrous roots around the outside, and cut into smaller pieces before drying. The root will smell unpleasant so it is not recommended to dry it in your home.

USES

For hundreds of years valerian has been a staple of herbal remedies for insomnia and anxiety, with the dried root used in small amounts in tea or in tinctures to soothe and sedate, though there is little scientific evidence of its efficacy.

The root and leaves are used in the garden in preparations for plant feed and to attract earthworms. The flowers bring a sweet fragrance to the house as cut flowers and are often used for dried arrangements. Cats love the smell of valerian root even more than catmint, and will come running when you dig it up.

VERVAIN *VERBENA OFFICINALIS*

Tall and spindly, vervain has lots of wiry branching stems topped with spikes of many small, pale lilac flowers. The foliage is glossy and green with divided, lobed leaves with roundly serrated edges; these are bigger and more densely arranged toward the base of the plant.

PLANT TYPE Herbaceous perennial
HARDINESS Hardy
HEIGHT Up to 3 ft (1 m)
SPREAD Up to 29 in (75 cm)
SOIL Any well-drained soil
LIGHT ☼

GROW AND MAINTAIN

Verbena officinalis has many common names including vervain, holy herb, pigeon grass, enchanter's balm, and simpler's joy, no doubt resulting from its reputation in folk tales as being effectively used to ward off the supernatural, and also as a cure-all. It is not a native plant but it has naturalized outside the garden and can also be found growing in places like road verges and brownfield sites.

The mauve-colored blooms appear in midsummer, opening from the bottom of the spike to the top over

The flowers of vervain are small and delicate, but rich in nectar.

time. They last up until mid-fall, and are a magnet for pollinators as they are packed with nectar.

For more visual impact in the garden, there is a widely available cultivar called *V. officinalis* var. *grandiflora* 'Bampton', which is taller and broader with pinky-purple blooms, and bronze- or purple-tinged foliage.

Grow in fertile, moist but well-drained soil in full sun. To start, sow indoors in early spring into trays or plugs of seed starting mix. Place somewhere bright and prick out and pot on seedlings once they are large enough to handle. Once all risk of frost has passed, harden off plants, placing them outside during the day and bringing them back in at night for about 10 days. Plant out in their final position spaced 12 in (30 cm) apart. Plant in groups for best effect. You can also sow seeds directly where they are to grow

Vervain has an open, airy habit with flowers borne on stiff, slender stems.

USES

Dried vervain leaves can be used in herbal teas, and the plant is often processed into an herbal supplement that is claimed to treat nervous conditions. The best use for it, however, is to attract pollinators like bees and butterflies into the garden, and as an airy cut flower for the house.

once all risk of frost has passed, or buy plants. Vervain does not do well when planted in containers.

Although quite drought-tolerant, keep plants well-watered while they establish. Deadhead flower heads or cut back the whole plant after flowering to prevent it from self-seeding.

Vervain can suffer if cut down in the fall, so leave top growth over winter and cut down to near the base once fresh growth appears in spring. Mulch to offer extra winter protection.

PROPAGATE Dig up a clump and divide in spring or fall. If you allow vervain to go to seed, many seedlings will spring up at the base, and you can then transplant them elsewhere.

HARVEST

Leaves can be picked as required throughout the season. Flower stems can be harvested while in bloom.

VIOLET *VIOLA*

Violets are grown for their pretty looks and edible blooms. They have small flowers in shades of purple, blue, or white, sometimes marked with yellow, and green heart-shaped or lobed leaves. The flowers appear in early spring or summer; some are highly fragrant with a sweet, powdery scent.

PLANT TYPE Evergreen or semi-evergreen perennial or annual
HARDINESS Hardy
HEIGHT Up to 8 in (20 cm)
SPREAD Up to 12 in (30 cm)
SOIL Any moist, well-drained soil
LIGHT ☼ ☼

GROW AND MAINTAIN

Sweet violet, *Viola odorata*, also known as wood violet, is a pretty perennial with semi-evergreen, rounded leaves and scented, deep purple-blue or white flowers. It is often seen in woodland and makes a good ground cover for shady areas. There are hybrid types available called parma violets.

Heartsease violas have appealing multi-colored flower heads.

Heartsease, *Viola tricolor*, also known as wild pansy, is not scented and has flowers with several colors of petals, and sometimes markings that make the blooms look like a face with whiskers. The flowers appear over a long period through summer, and look cheery in a container. It is an evergreen perennial but is often grown as an annual or biennial, as it can be quite short-lived.

Grow sweet violet in moist, rich, well-drained soil in part shade. Heartsease will grow in any well-drained soil in sun or part-shade.

The seed is not easy to germinate. If you would like to try, order fresh seed in summer and sow in late summer or fall into trays of seed starting mix. Leave somewhere protected, but not warm, over winter—such as a cold frame—as the seeds need a period of cold to sprout. In spring, once seedlings are large enough to handle, they can be pricked out and potted up to grow on, before being planted out where they are to grow. Alternatively, buy pot-grown plants in spring. Space plants around 12 cm (30 cm) apart.

Keep them well-watered, and watch out for damage from slugs and snails. Deadhead the flowers or pick regularly to encourage more to form. Mulch to retain moisture and help enrich the soil.

PROPAGATE Established plants can be divided in spring. Violets will self-sow, and also spread via runners on the surface of the soil, like strawberries do—these can be removed in spring.

USES

Both species of violets have edible flowers that can be added to salads, or used fresh or crystallized (candied) to decorate cakes and garnish desserts and drinks. Sweet violet is the main flavor in violet cream candies. Its leaves can also be eaten like spinach.

Crystallized violets make the prettiest and sweetest of decorations for cakes and desserts.

PRUNE To keep a compact shape, clip back all over after flowering to 2 in (5 cm) from the base.

HARVEST

Pick sweet violets and heartsease flowers when they have just opened.

MONK'S PEPPER

VITEX AGNUS-CASTUS

This large, vase-shaped shrub is a great late-season nectar source for pollinators such as butterflies. It has maplelike palmate leaves, which are green and aromatic. In the fall, it produces spikes of small purple-blue to lavender-colored flowers at the end of its stems, followed by orange berries.

PLANT TYPE Deciduous shrub
HARDINESS Half hardy
HEIGHT Up to 6½ ft (2m)
SPREAD Up to 6½ ft (2m)
SOIL Any well-drained soil
LIGHT ☼
WARNING! Should not be ingested during pregnancy

Vitex agnus-castus **f. *latifolia*** has very fragrant flowers in the fall.

Monk's pepper berries are produced in warmer climates and used as a spice.

GROW AND MAINTAIN

Monk's pepper, *Vitex agnus-castus*, is also known as chaste tree, as it was thought to quell lustful urges. It is a bushy, fragrant plant with an open, spreading habit, and grows fast, becoming just as wide as it is tall. Types include DELTA BLUES, which flowers early, from late spring or early summer to late summer; BLUE PUFFBALL is small, to just 3 ft (1 m); and the white-flowered *V. agnus-castus* f. *alba* and its cultivar 'Silver Spire'. *V. agnus-castus* f. *latifolia* is the broad-leaved variety, with pleasingly scented purple blooms.

It is probably best to buy a young pot-grown plant, because it can take more than five years for a plant to mature and flower if it is grown from seed. Moreover, the seed has to be perfectly fresh when sown and is not widely available in this form.

Native to the Mediterranean, it likes a warm and fairly dry spot. It can suffer from dieback in very harsh winters, and won't produce berries in cold climates, though it can handle temperatures down to 23 to 14°F (−5 to −10°C). Give it a sheltered position out of the wind, ideally against a south- or west-facing wall, in full sun. Plant out in the garden in spring after all risk of frost, in any well-drained soil. It hates sitting in wet, heavy soils, especially in winter.

Monk's pepper can also be grown in a large container if fed and watered regularly through summer. Make sure the container has good drainage in winter by setting the pot on feet.

PROPAGATE The easiest way to propagate is to take softwood cuttings in spring, or semi-hardwood (semi-ripe) cuttings in summer. If your plant sets berries, collect and try sowing the inner seed fresh in the fall.

PRUNE Prune each spring once established. Clip back stems to within 2 in (5 cm) of the previous season's growth. Alternatively, to keep this vigorous grower in check, hard prune the branches back to 12–20 in (30–50 cm) from the base annually.

HARVEST

The berries should be harvested when ripe, and then dried before use. Pick leaves before flowering, when young.

USES

The berries can be dried and ground up to replace pepper in cooking, and are a core ingredient of most *ras el hanout* spice mixes, used in North African dishes. The leaves, which smell like sage, can be dried and used as seasoning.

Monk's pepper is a traditional herbal remedy for female fertility and menstrual issues, but it should not be taken during pregnancy.

WASABI *WASABIA JAPONICA*

Wasabi, also known as Japanese horseradish, has big, lily pad–like green leaves on long stalks, and clusters of small white flowers in spring. However, it is grown for its "root"—a thick rhizome or underground stem that has a hot, mustardy flavor without spice, similar to that of horseradish.

PLANT TYPE Evergreen perennial
HARDINESS Hardy
HEIGHT 24 in (60 cm)
SPREAD Up to 3 ft (1 m)
SOIL Any moist, well-drained soil
LIGHT ☼ ☀

Wasabi's striking foliage is produced from early spring to late fall.

GROW AND MAINTAIN

Wasabia japonica is very popular in Japan, where it is grown for its rhizomes, often in stream-side locations under evergreen forest canopies. It makes a striking garden plant, with its large heart- or kidney-shaped foliage and scented spring blooms.

It requires a position in the shade, in rich, moist soil. It is not an aquatic plant, but a damp yet well-drained situation, for example the banks of a pond, is ideal. Wasabi likes cool climates. It will tolerate cold down to 23°F (–5°C), but will grow best where temperatures stay above 45°F (7°C) in winter and below around 73°F (23°C) in summer.

Most seeds with the word "wasabi" on the packet are actually types of arugula or mustard that are grown for hot leaves, and not real wasabi, so it is

The green "root" of wasabi is best used as fresh as possible after harvesting.

best to buy small plants in spring or early fall. Plant in a small container of potting mix to grow on for around a month. If planting in spring, make sure to harden off plants, after all risk of frost, before planting out.

Prepare the ground by digging in organic matter (such as garden compost) to enrich the soil and improve drainage. Dig a hole slightly larger than the plant's root ball, and place it in so the crown (where the underground part of the plant meets the section that grows above ground) is sitting just above the soil surface. Space plants at least 12 in (30 cm) apart. Water in well.

Keep the soil moist and feed regularly with a general purpose liquid fertilizer in spring and summer. Watch out for damage from slugs. Mulch to protect over winter and use horticultural fleece if very cold weather is forecast.

PROPAGATE If happy, wasabi may well self-seed, but a successful method is to look out for small off-shoots growing on established plants, which you can remove and pot up to grow on.

HARVEST

From two months after planting, you can pick leaves and stems—sparingly at first. Always leave the small leaf coming out of the middle of the plant. The spring after planting, you can pick the white flowers. Harvest the rhizomes two years after planting. Dig up just one first to check the size: they should be around 8 in (20 cm) long. Take off the leaves and hairy roots, and clean off the soil. You can store it wrapped in damp paper towel, in a plastic food storage bag in the fridge for several weeks.

USES

The rhizome is grated or ground and added to water to make a paste, or mixed with sauces like mayonnaise, dips, and dressings to create piquant condiments for sushi, sashimi, vegetable and meat dishes, noodles, and soups. The leaves can be used like spinach, raw or cooked. The stalks can be used like celery, and are particularly good chopped up in mashed potatoes. The flowers can be added raw to salads or made into a tasty tempura.

GINGER *ZINGIBER OFFICINALE*

Ginger is a tropical plant with narrow, lance-shaped leaves on either side of tall stems, and yellow and purple flowers in a dense spike or cone. It is grown for its pinky-brown rhizome, which has a yellow center that tastes and smells pungently like spicy citrus.

PLANT TYPE Deciduous perennial
HARDINESS Tender
HEIGHT Up to 6 ft (1.2 m)
SPREAD Up to 24 in (60 cm)
SOIL Light, well-drained soil
LIGHT ☼ ◖

GROW AND MAINTAIN

Ginger originates from Southeast Asia, and likes warm and moist conditions. Although it does have attractive flowers and bracts, these are not likely to be produced in colder regions. It will not withstand frost or winters outside in cooler climates, so grow in a container, which can be placed outside in summer, but brought indoors as temperatures drop in fall. It may prefer to be under cover all year.

Grow in rich, fertile, potting soil. These plants like bright light, such as full sun outdoors in a cool-climate summer, but should not be placed in direct sunlight when growing under glass, where diffused sun or part shade is best.

You can order ginger rhizomes to plant or try to grow from a supermarket "root." Only use organic ginger, as many non-organic ones are treated with a growth inhibitor that will prevent them from sprouting. An overnight soaking will remove the growth inhibitor.

In early spring, pick a rhizome that looks plump and healthy. Think of it as a hand with fingers, each with a knobbly growth eye or bud (these may be green if really fresh). Cut it up into the individual fingers with a sharp knife, and let the pieces sit and dry out for a day. Plant them into small pots of warm potting mix, placing them just under the surface, with the growth eyes or buds pointing up. Place in a heated propagator or cover with a clear plastic bag and place somewhere warm and bright, like a windowsill. Water sparingly, with tepid, not cold, water for a few weeks, until shoots appear. Take it out of the propagator or bag. After another few weeks, you can pot up into its larger growing container. If you are placing your ginger outdoors in summer, give it a sheltered position out of the wind. Keep it moist but ensure it has good drainage. Bring the pot back inside once the temperature drops to around 50°F (10°C) at night in the fall. Plants will die back and you can cut down the old stems. Repot into a larger container once it has filled the pot.

PROPAGATE When harvesting your ginger rhizome, break off a section with leaves attached and replant immediately to grow on.

Ginger produces attractive foliage but may not flower in cooler regions.

USES

Ginger adds a spicy kick to both savory and sweet dishes. Dried and powdered or preserved in sugar, it is used in desserts, drinks, and baked goods like cookies, tea, ginger beer, gingerbread, and jams. The fresh "root" is mild and succulent in flavor and texture, but as it dries and matures it gets hotter and more fibrous. It is used in many Asian cuisines, chopped or grated, to add fire to stir fries, marinades, and sauces, and pickled as a condiment.

Ginger can be used fresh, or dried and then ground to powder.

HARVEST

Harvest the "root" about 10 months after planting. Carefully dig around the rhizome and lift the plant. Remove the stems and clean the rhizome. Use fresh, grating or slicing only what you need, or pop into a food storage bag in your fridge. For long-term storage, keep in the freezer in an airtight container.

INDEX

Bold text indicates a main entry for the subject.

Author Stephanie Mahon

AUTHOR ACKNOWLEDGMENTS
I would like to thank Marek and Paul at Cobalt id and Sarah for her fine editing work, and John C for all the cups of tea.

PUBLISHER ACKNOWLEDGMENTS
DK would like to thank Mary-Clare Jerram for developing the original concept; John Tullock for consulting; Margaret McCormack for indexing; and Paul Reid, Marek Walisiewicz, and the Cobalt team for their hard work in putting this book together.

PICTURE CREDITS
The publisher would like to thank the following for their kind permission to reproduce their photographs:

Alamy Stock Photo: Imagebroker 130r; agefotostock 59br, 139c; alicja neumiler 10tr; Anett Bulano 77l; Avalon.red 81tl; Bailey-Cooper Photography 100cr; blickwinkel 82r, 90r, 137bl; Botanic World 38br, 111rc; Brent Hofacker 11cr; Brian Hird (Wildflowers) 103c; Burke's Backyard 4l; Cavan Images 97bc; Chris Dennis 83l; Clare Gainey 121tc; Cultura Creative RF 53b; D. Hurst 46tr; David Chapman 25br; Deborah Vernon 11br; Delphine Adburgham 71lc; Denis Crawford 35br; Derek Harris 22bl; Design Pics 60c; Elena Elisseeva 52cr, 141cr; Emilio Ereza 109bc; es-cuisine/PhotoAlto 138cr; Fir Mamat 127c; floricos 109tl; flowerphotos 79c, 127l; FLPA 43bl; Geo-grafika 81br; GKSFlorapics 23tr, 123l; Graham Martin 75l; Ilia Nesolenyi 47br; Image Professionals GmbH 126br; Irina Naoumova 80l; James Jenkins - Natural History Photography 24tr; John Glover 25bc; Jolanta Dąbrowska 71bc; Kay Fochtmann 13tl; lee avison 133bl; Leszek Kobusinski 78cr; Manfred Ruckszio 141bl; Manuel Tauber-Romieri 55br; mauritius images GmbH 69rc; mediasculp 43tl, 119bc; Nobuo Matsumura 102tc; Norbert-Zsolt Suto 86r; Panther Media GmbH 78bl; Photononstop 28cl; QxQ images 105t; RM Floral 118c, 129c; Rob Walls 113l; robertharding 86l; Sabena Jane Blackbird 74r; Snow white Images 102tl; Steffen Hauser / botanikfoto 64l, 69bl; STUDIO75 94l; TG23 23tl; The National Trust Photolibrary 65c; Tim Hill 68rc; Tommi Syvänperä 84r; Viktor Löki 123bc; Zoltan Bagosi 120bl; Zoonar GmbH 34bl; McPhoto/Rolf Mueller 124l.

Dorling Kindersley: Mark Winwood / Downderry Nursery 96c, 96rc, 97tr; Mark Winwood / Hampton Court Flower Show 2014 93l, 133cr; Mark Winwood / RHS Malvern Flower Show 2014 110bc, 110br; Mark Winwood / RHS Wisley 29cl, 51tr, 100c, 110bl, 111tl, 111tr, 119tl, 139cl, RHS Wisley 120c.

GAP Photos: 25tc, 25tr, 25c, 25cr, 40bl, 41cl, 41c, 41br, 63tc; Carole Drake 22cr; Friedrich Strauss 16cl; Gary Smith 33tc; Jo Whitworth 73tr; John Swithinbank 38cl; Jonathan Buckley 39tl; Lee Avison 13bc; Nicola Stocken 24bc, 46br.

Getty Images: Andres Jacobi 10bl; Chris Griffiths 20br; Cyndi Monaghan 66r; Julija Kumpinovica 2c; kirin_photo 11cl; Les Hirondelles Photography 11bl; mrybski 72b; sauletas 81tr.

Illustrations by Cobalt id.

All other images © Dorling Kindersley

Produced for DK by
COBALT ID

Managing Editor Marek Walisiewicz
Editor Sarah Mitchell
Managing Art Editor Paul Reid
Art Editor Darren Bland

DK LONDON
Project Editor Amy Slack
US Editor Megan Douglass
Managing Editor Ruth O'Rourke
Managing Art Editors Christine Keilty, Marianne Markham
Production Editor David Almond
Senior Production Controller Stephanie McConnell
Jacket Designers Nicola Powling, Amy Cox
Jacket Coordinator Lucy Philpott
Consultant Gardening Publisher Chris Young
Art Director Maxine Pedliham
Publishers Katie Cowan

First American Edition, 2022
Published in the United States by DK Publishing
1450 Broadway, Suite 801, New York, NY 10018

Copyright © 2022 Dorling Kindersley Limited
DK, a Division of Penguin Random House LLC
21 22 23 24 25 10 9 8 7 6 5 4 3 2 1
001–326202–Apr/2022

A catalog record for this book
is available from the Library of Congress.
ISBN 978-0-7440-4813-1

DK books are available at special discounts when purchased in bulk for sales promotions, premiums, fund-raising, or educational use. For details, contact:
DK Publishing Special Markets, 1450 Broadway, Suite 801, New York, NY 10018
SpecialSales@dk.com

Printed and bound in China

For the curious
www.dk.com